0123 WH

# CHATHAM
## SEA CAPTAINS
### IN THE AGE OF SAIL

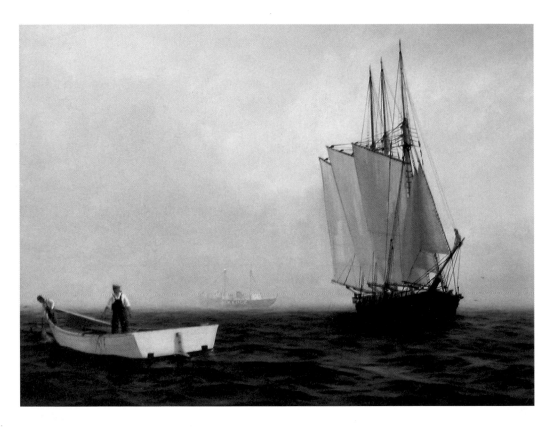

Jeff Eldredge's painting, a portion of which appears on the cover, illustrates an event in author Joe Nickerson's life, when out fishing with his father off Pollack Rip Lightship, a classic schooner came sailing out of the fog. Joe grew up hearing the tales of Chatham's sea captains from his father's knee. As a member of Chatham's founding family, young Joe knew many of the sea captains who sailed into the 20th Century.

# CHATHAM
# SEA CAPTAINS
## IN THE AGE OF SAIL

JOSEPH A. NICKERSON JR. & GERALDINE D. NICKERSON

Charleston ⎯ London

History
PRESS

Published by The History Press
Charleston, SC 29403
www.historypress.net

*Cover:* A three-masted schooner emerges from the fog off Chatham, making her way south in this portion of a painting by Jeff Eldredge. *Joseph A. Nickerson Jr. Collection.*
*Back:* Captain Elijah Crosby (1819–1898).

First published 2008

Manufactured in the United Kingdom

ISBN 978.1.59629.431.8

Library of Congress Cataloging-in-Publication Data

Nickerson, Joseph A., Jr.
Chatham sea captains in the age of sail / Joseph A. Nickerson Jr. and
Geraldine D. Nickerson ; edited by Janet Daly.
p. cm.
Includes bibliographical references and index.
ISBN-13: 978-1-59629-431-8 (alk. paper)
1. Ship captains--Massachusetts--Chatham--Biography. 2.
Navigation--Massachusetts--Chatham--History. 3. Chatham (Mass.)--Biography.
I. Nickerson, Geraldine D. II. Daly, Janet. III. Title.
VK139.N53 2008
387.5092'274492--dc22
                                    2007046896

*Notice*: The information in this book is true and complete to the best of our knowledge. It is offered without guarantee on the part of the author or The History Press. The author and The History Press disclaim all liability in connection with the use of this book.

*This book honors the memory of A. Louise Wentworth Nickerson for her untiring dedication in documenting the lives of Chatham's sea captains.*

# CONTENTS

**Part III: Sailing into the Twentieth Century**

# FOREWORD

*Chatham Sea Captains in the Age of Sail* could only have been created by someone who has spent nearly his entire life studying, researching and collecting every available archive that relates to the history of Chatham—in this instance, that someone is Joseph Atkins Nickerson Jr. While many of the descendants of William Nickerson, the founder of Chatham, have an intense interest in the history of the town and its people, few—if any—have dedicated so many years to learning everything possible about it.

It is because of the depth and breadth of this interest that Joe began, along with his first wife Louise more than thirty-five years ago, to collect letters, diaries, logbooks, newspaper articles and any other material relating to the sea captains of Chatham. With the encouragement and assistance of his present wife Geraldine, Joe devoted the past several years to reviewing, selecting and organizing the particular documents that have become the body of this magnificent work.

The result of those labors is this lively, readable, intriguing and fascinating account of the experiences of some of the sea captains represented in the Nickersons's wealth of documents. To read this book is the closest we in the twenty-first century can ever come to sailing the seas in the age of sail. We become acquainted with not only the grueling labors and the hardships faced by those who ply the seas, but also with the ingenuity and courage required of them. Moreover we come to understand the involvement of their families, whether waiting patiently—yet often fearfully—at home, or bracing the seas to be at the side of their men.

In this unique book we are given so many firsthand accounts of those experiences that we feel almost as if we know intimately the captains, their families and their crews. Beyond that, we learn about their social conditions and mores, as well as about their interaction with other societies throughout the world from their accounts of visits to Europe, South America, the South Seas, the Orient and Australia.

The Chatham Historical Society is indebted to Joe and Gerry Nickerson for making this superb work available to all who are interested in the history of our town and its people. It is indeed a valuable and important addition to the available accounts of our heritage.

Spencer Y. Grey
Chairman, Chatham Historical Society

# ACKNOWLEDGEMENTS

Our book stems from thirty-five years of research—years of intensive, single-minded activity on the part of Joe and his first wife, Louise. They sought information about Chatham master mariners, sea captains and even lesser mariners in libraries, vital records and old newspapers of the time, as well as through recollections of old-timers and their own contemporaries who remembered some of the old sea captains and their families. Their search took them to every available source on Cape Cod, in New England and beyond.

*Chatham Sea Captains in the Age of Sail* relies on the above research, but it is not intended to be an account of all the mariners who ever called Chatham their home. Rather, we wish to introduce you to a number of the more interesting shipmasters, who represent so many others. We hope these profiles will make them, and the "age of sail," come alive today.

Joe's sons, Joseph III and Steven, gave us valuable suggestions as to the content. Steven, Kenney, Robert and Peter guided me in my indoctrination into the "briar patch" of the computer world.

We also thank Joe's daughters, Donna and Wendy, and the many friends who have encouraged and reassured us along the way.

First and foremost has been Spencer Y. Grey, longtime enthusiast for all things historical, who has been supportive of this project from its very beginning.

Rob Carlisle was generous with his time and advice at the outset of this writing.

Florine and Dwight Myer gave valuable assistance with research at the Atwood House Museum.

We extend our thanks to Mrs. James Hardy for photographs and to Robert Hardy for logs of his great-grandfather, Josiah Hardy.

The greatest assist, without which this project could never have seen the light of day, has been given us by Janet M. Daly, our editor and friend. It is her enthusiasm, expertise and her generous sharing of time and energy that have made this material into a book. Without Janet, we might still just be *hoping* to see these words in print!

Geraldine D. Nickerson

North Chatham, Massachusetts

October 2007

# INTRODUCTION

Shipowners and merchants sought Chatham sea captains for their superior seamanship, integrity, resourcefulness and dependability. Their reputation went far beyond Cape Cod. The son of one eminent Boston owner/merchant is quoted thus:

> *When we still owned ships, so far as possible, we chose Chatham or Cape men as masters. The choice was based upon the confidence and belief in the character and ability of the men.*[1]

Fledgling sea captains grew up in a village where going to sea was a way of life. They learned respect for the sea as a force to be reckoned with, in good weather or bad—as the treacherous shoals surrounding Chatham's harbors taught them only too well. The sea was both foe and ally. To meet the foe was the challenge; to sail her waters and return home as true masters was the force that drove them to excellence.

The sea captains we selected for this book illustrate three well-defined areas in which our Chatham men excelled: as deep-sea captains who fished the Grand Banks of Nova Scotia; as coastal or packet skippers who carried goods to Atlantic ports and as far as the West Indies; and as masters of the Seven Seas who went far afield—to Europe, Africa, South America, Asia and the "Down Under."

## Deep-Sea Captains

Deep-sea fishermen were independent. They did not take kindly to the rigid, often cruel discipline exacted from crewmen on big vessels that engaged in foreign trade. Deep-sea captains were in business for themselves. They—as well as their crews—tended to belong to family groups. The Bloomer captains, for example, chose the comradeship of six or eight men on their relatively small two- or three-masted fishing schooners. They

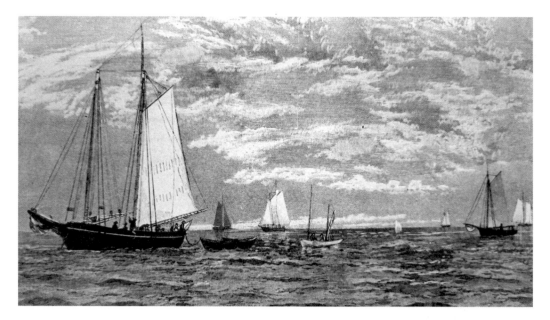

A fishing fleet creates a community of schooners with their dories as they fish on the banks off the East Coast of the United States. *Joseph A. Nickerson Collection.*

were handline fishermen who braved the dangers and hardships of the Grand Banks and Newfoundland. They fished in the fall and winter when ice, snow, howling winds and fog made fishing treacherous. Kipling's book title, *Captains Courageous*, says it all.

Their catches were salted or dried and taken either to European ports or brought home for distribution up and down the Atlantic coast, even as far as the West Indies. Deep-sea fishing occupied just six months of rigorous toil, after which the men stayed home with their families for the remainder of the year. This gave them time to repair their boats and gear, plant the family gardens in the spring, harvest them and then in mid-October, sail away in company with a score of friendly schoonermen from their own and nearby ports.

There was a closeness in the society of skippers on the Grand Banks (also called the "Blue Water"). If a schooner was in trouble and needed supplies or help in the event of injury, comrades were close at hand to help. Mary Ellen Chase, in her book *The Fishing Fleets of New England*, speaks of this camaraderie as exemplifying "democracy at its best and noblest off those foggy northern coasts."

## The Coastal Captains

Our second category includes those men who chose coastal commerce. These captains and crews were able to be in closer contact with their families and friends. Captains such as Darius Hammond and Reuben Taylor were primarily masters of coastal freighters that traveled from one specific port to another. These vessels belonged generally to a merchant, a group of investors or a shipping company, such as the Dispatch Line.

Usually the captains went where the owners had contracted cargo. The vessels carried in their holds lumber, machinery, coal and other such items.

Speedy packets also became a part of coastal merchandizing. To this group belong captains of "coasties"—vessels that plied the East Coast, trading here and there but without an assigned cargo or port of call. These captains were generally owners of their cargoes, and were frequently either full or part owners of their brigs or small schooners as well. They were actively engaged in buying what they carried, selling it and then buying other commodities to bring back for sale at their home ports. Such Chatham men as the Pattersons belong in this category. A great many had specific runs—from Boston to New York or Philadelphia, or down to Mobile and New Orleans.

When the ships returned with great treasures from the Orient, it was the coastal vessels' turn to distribute this bounty. In many respects, the coastal vessels and the captains who sailed them fulfilled a need that could not be met by other means.

America's Industrial Revolution—noteworthy particularly in the New England states—owes much of its success to these same shipmasters. Their barks and schooners, with ample holds, brought millions of bales of cotton from Alabama and South Carolina for the manufacture of cloth made here in New England's New Bedford, Fall River and Lowell mills. Vast quantities of coal from West Virginia and Pennsylvania were brought to fuel this revolution. This trade was a significant factor in the advancement of the country, with its promise of economic growth and a greatly improved physical comfort for its people.

## Masters of the Seven Seas

The length of their voyages, their relatively large vessels, the extent of the territory they covered and the wealth they amassed in their journeys characterized Chatham captains in this third group. The world was their oyster and their rewards were great indeed.

Generally speaking, their barks, brigs, schooners and ships were built to accommodate large amounts of freight. The advent of the clipper ships in the 1840s and 1850s provided an element of speed, but with less space for freight than the later four-, five- and six-masted schooners.

The captains brought lumber, salt cod, tobacco and other New World products to Mediterranean ports and North Africa and returned with such delicacies as oranges, figs, lemons, nuts and olive oil. This "fruit trade," as it was called, brought unusual foods to New England tables and beyond for the first time. There were exotic woods from South America and Asia—mahogany and teak, which enriched the homes, churches and other public buildings in this country. Other ships brought less exotic cargo from South America—guano, for instance, which might not be an appealing cargo, but was a necessary one.

When gold was discovered in California, the rush was on and the clipper ship beauties with their enormous sails were the transportation of choice. Passengers, and cargo to feed, clothe and equip the miners, all sailed around Cape Horn as fast as they could. Races between shipmasters were notable, and these vessels garnered higher rates that brought not only fame to their owners, but fortunes as well.

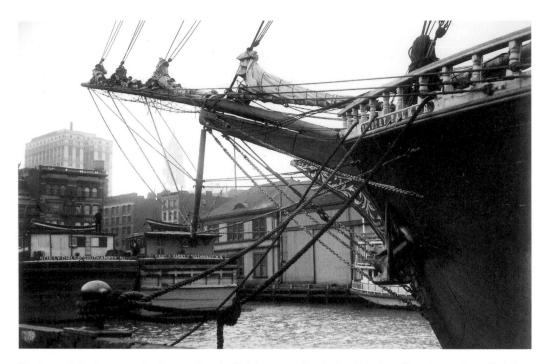

The bow of the five-masted schooner *Dorothy B. Palmer* at anchor in Perth Amboy, New Jersey. She sailed the seas for twenty years until she went down off Handkerchief Shoals on Cape Cod. *Joseph A. Nickerson Collection.*

Sea captains who took their vessels to Australia and New Zealand for enormous quantities of wool brought these riches back to be manufactured into blankets, fabrics and woolen clothing in mills along the Connecticut River valley, fueling New England's industrialization. Their many masted schooners were frequent visitors to ports throughout the world.

Those who ventured to Australia, New Zealand, Singapore, the Philippines, China, India and Japan belong to an elite group of Chatham sea captains. Although "China Trade" is a term loosely associated with this third group, it would be incorrect to give the impression that all of these great masters were involved with it. To men such as Benajah Crowell Jr., David Smith or Hiram Harding, for example, China Trade would not apply.

Today, these captains are considered the elite of Chatham master mariners. To their credit, no such pretensions were ever voiced by them. Many Chatham captains were educated men, with a breadth of knowledge and interest in literary and artistic matters. To their competency as masters must be added a shrewd Yankee business sense and the ability to negotiate effectively.

## Chatham's Sea Captains

All of these Chatham sea captains were at home on the sea. Whether it was off the Grand Banks or close to Cape shores, skirting Cape Horn or rounding the Cape of

Good Hope, they knew the sting of wind-driven rain and icy gales and hurricanes. During both the eighteenth and nineteenth centuries they were prey to privateers, unfriendly naval vessels and even pirates. Impressment was a strong possibility during the War of 1812, and Confederate raiders sought them out during the Civil War.

For these men drawn to the sea as by a siren call—men who loved the feel of a worthy craft under them and the thrill of meeting and conquering the sea in all of her moods— there were no other endeavors equal to that. We believe Chatham's master mariners personify the best of New England's men of any generation. As Alpheus Hardy once said to a Chatham captain, "I have not chartered your vessel, but you."[2]

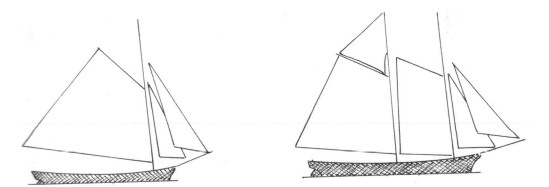

A sloop, *left*, has a single mast, rigged fore and aft, closer to the bow. A schooner, *right*, has two masts, rigged fore and aft. The aft mast is the same size or larger than the foremast. *Drawings by Jeff Eldredge.*

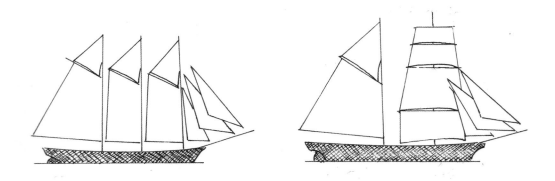

A tern schooner, *left*, has three masts. A half brig, also called a hermaphrodite brig or brig-schooner, *right*, has two masts with square sails on the foremast with schooner rig on the mainmast—note the triangular topsail over the gaff mainsail. *Drawings by Jeff Eldredge.*

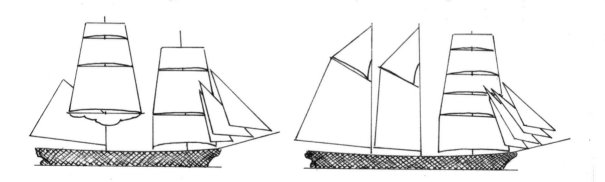

A brig, *left*, has two square-rigged masts. A barkentine, *right*, has three or more masts with a square-rigged foremast and only fore and aft rigged on the mainmast, mizzenmast and any other masts. *Drawings by Jeff Eldredge.*

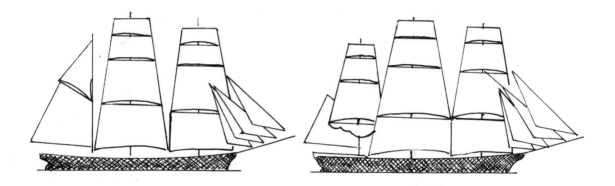

Barks, *left*, have three or more masts, foresails and aft sails on the aftermost mast and square sails on all others. A ship, *right*, has three or more masts, all with yardarms. Other masts may be fore and aft rigged. *Drawings by Jeff Eldredge.*

# *Part I*
# COLONIAL AND EARLY AMERICAN CAPTAINS

# JOSEPH ATWOOD
## (1720–1794)
### *Navigator of Unfrequented Ports*

T he Atwood homestead—today the home of the Chatham Historical Society on Stage Harbor Road—was built by Captain Joseph Atwood in 1752. It was one of the most expensive houses of its day and remains one of the finest specimens of Colonial architecture on Cape Cod. If only Captain Atwood could come back to life and see the house in its present, lovingly preserved and expanded state as the core of the remarkable Atwood House Museum!

Captain Atwood was able to afford such a home because of his success as a sea captain. He probably went to sea when he was about ten years old, and learned the ways of the sea on the fishing vessels that went to Nova Scotia and the Grand Banks.

> *In the old days, a boy would take to the sea as naturally as a duck takes to water, and ships and the sea would constitute his life work. Moreover, from the start of his career, he was more or less a partner in every marine venture; there was no tradition to cramp, stifle, or swamp him—no class distinction and limitation as in Europe; he was the master of his own fate and free to carve out a future for himself that could be anything hard work, self-sacrifice, developed talents, and proven ability could produce. The colonial and early American fisheries gave to the United States its greatest sailors and the forebears of its outstanding shipmasters.*[1]

The deep-sea captains not only caught cod, but they also preserved and delivered it to market. The dry fishery method saw boats return to shore to salt and dry the cod on flakes. In the wet fishery method, cod was caught, salted and stored on board, then taken to ports along the eastern coast of North America as far south as the West Indies, or directly to Europe. Many young men became masters of their own vessels before they were twenty-five years old.

That seems to have been the case with Captain Atwood, according to this excerpt from *The History of Chatham* by William C. Smith:

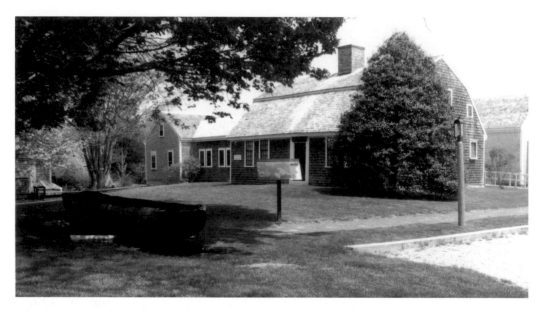

Captain Atwood's "mansion," a full Cape with gambrel roof, is the heart of the Chatham Historical Society's Atwood House Museum in Chatham, Massachusetts. *Joseph A. Nickerson Jr. Collection.*

*About 1740 Chatham men began to secure command of vessels sailing to the West Indies and to European ports, though both were then rather hazardous trips. Captain Joseph Atwood was one of the first of these captains, sailing in command of ships owned by Boston parties. He made several voyages in the snow[2] Judith, a square-sterned ship of 80 tons, to the Bay of Honduras and thence to Amsterdam and back. In the schooner* Isle Sables Galley, *he went to England, Amsterdam and back in 1747. At other times he commanded the sloop* Falmouth.

*The Cape Cod Pilot*, by Jeremiah Digges, offers the following information about the captain:

*Captain Joseph Atwood was an Eastham man[3], a "navigator of unfrequented parts" according to the family records. When he was skippering the snow* Judith, *in 1749…his Boston owners gave him the following orders to cheer him on his way: "While you are out lest you be overpowered by Spaniards, and as you are well fitted for defense[4] we expect you to put up a manly defense in case you are attacked."*

*With a set of orders such as these to give him instructions, it is little wonder that the skipper went home to find a "snug harbor" as soon as he could scrape up the price. He was too good a Yankee to run risks for nothing. He retired with what in those days was a fortune. He went back to Colonel Doane, who owned everything for miles around, and bought 30 acres in Monomoy [now Chatham]. In 1752, he came here [Chatham] and built his "Mansion House," as the little cottage was referred to in his will, a gambrel-roofed house, still called "the old Atwood House."*

This Bible page records the Atwood children's births— Bethiah, David, Deborah, Joseph, Sears and Sarah —and the deaths of Joseph and Sarah. The captain and his wife Deborah's deaths are at the end. *Courtesy, of the Chatham (MA) Historical Society, Inc.*

Captain Atwood sailed to Nova Scotia, Liverpool and Amsterdam and back in 1747 as master of the *Isle Sables Galley*, named for the island off Nova Scotia in the heart of the fishing grounds. Seldom do we find accounts of how many men comprised the crew in the mid-1700s, so we were surprised to read that the crews of the *Isle Sables Galley* and the *Falmouth* were captain, mate and three or four sailors. Such a list indicates how comparatively small these vessels were.

When the *Judith* sailed into Boston on February 29, 1752, however, it had a crew of eleven in addition to the captain, first and second mates and the ship's carpenter. In 1768, Captain Atwood was transporting white pine boards, white pine shingles, clapboards and laths to Boston and thence to Chatham. It is likely that going out from Chatham and Boston to "unfrequented ports" the cargo contained tobacco and salt codfish, as well as furs, and upon return it contained tea, wines, silks, laces and other niceties from Amsterdam.

After retiring from sea, Captain Atwood became an important landowner and farmer. He owned extensive property on either side of what is now Stage Harbor Road and was a wealthy, highly respected member of the Chatham community. He was active in various pursuits, including some involved with the maritime trade. He lived a full, rich and eventful life.

In his will, he bequeathed to his wife Deborah, the "improvement of my Real Estate after debts are paid (except one-third part of my dwelling house) 2 good cows, my horse, 6 pigs, and the improvement of my household."

His son, Sears, received:

> *all real estate after my wife's decease and my just debts are paid (excepting one third of my dwelling) and my pew in the meeting house, allowing to my two daughters Deborah and Sarah to each the right to sit inside the pew during life—all my wearing apparel and all farming utensils. To daughter Sarah Atwood, one third of my dwelling house to be improved for as long as she shall remain unmarried.*

The family is interred in the Old South (Ancient) Cemetery located off Old Queen Anne Road, except for Sears, who was buried in 1832 in Union Cemetery.

Born a subject of the English monarchy, Captain Atwood died in his seventy-fourth year as a citizen of the world's newest democracy.

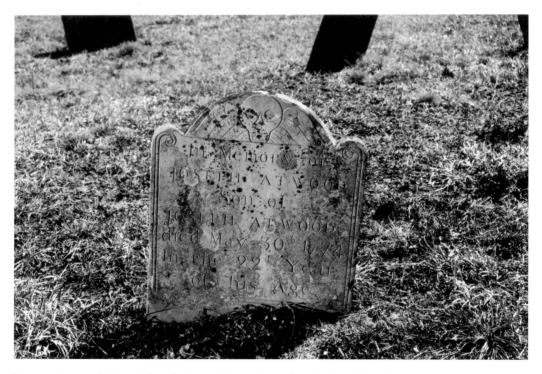

The tombstone of Captain Joseph Atwood shows signs of age in the Old South (Ancient) Cemetery off Old Queen Anne's Road in Chatham. *Courtesy of the Chatham (MA) Historical Society, Inc.*

# JOSEPH DOANE JR.
## (1744–1801)
### *Murder on the High Seas*

O ne of the most horrible sea mysteries that ever occurred on the East Coast remains unsolved after more than 230 years. Captain Joseph Doane Jr. played a key role in the tragedy. Here is how the story unfolds:[1]

*Captain Joseph Doane Jr. of Chatham was off the backside of the Cape in a schooner,[2] in 1772, and there sighted a vessel flying distress signals. Coming alongside, he found that she was the Schooner* Abigail, *Thomas Nickerson of Chatham, Master, outward bound from Boston, and a grim spectacle she presented. Her deck was smeared with blood. Capt. Nickerson, his cousin Sparrow Nickerson by name, and his brother-in-law, Elisha Newcomb, lay murdered on deck; chests were smashed open and rifled; a rum barrel with its head stove in stood almost empty; and only one man of the crew, Ansel Nickerson, of Chatham, was left alive on board.*

*According to him they had been overhauled the night before by a piratical topsail schooner which sent four boatloads of men on board. To save his own life, he had lowered himself over the taffrail* [at the stern of the ship] *on a rope and kept out of sight under the vessel's counter.*

*The pirates killed everyone on deck except a 13-year-old boy named William Kent Jr., whom, after helping themselves to the contents of the lockers and nearly finishing the barrel of rum, they had carried off with them. There had been some discussion, Nickerson said, as to whether or not they should burn the* Abigail, *but they left her as she was and put back to their own vessel, which was soon lost in the darkness.*

*This story sounded plausible enough to Captain Doane. He carried Nickerson back to Chatham and reported the occurrence to Edward Bacon, Esq., of Barnstable. Bacon sent a copy of the report to the Governor and straightway rode to Chatham to cross-question Nickerson. Apparently he was not satisfied with the result of the examination, for he had the man locked up in the Barnstable jail until further evidence should be forthcoming. Two frigates scoured the Sound in vain for any trace of the pirates, and Squire Bacon's suspicions increased. He sent his man in custody to Boston, where a special Court of Vice-Admiralty tried him for murder on the high seas.*

*The trial lasted for two weeks and rocked the town. John Adams and Josiah Quincy Jr. were counsel for the defense, and finally Nickerson was declared not guilty. Such, so far as they are known, are the facts in this strange tale of the sea. Let each decide for himself what happened or let him unearth more evidence if he can.*

Ansel Nickerson was last known to have left Chatham and settled on the island of Eleuthra, in the Bahamas.

When war broke out between the colonies and England, Captain Doane was already in the militia as an ensign in Captain Benjamin Godfrey's company at the siege of Boston. Later that year, he became second officer on the sloop *Wolf*, which was among those captured by a British man-of-war disguised as a merchant ship. He was sent to New York to prison but never got that far and was exchanged at Newport, Rhode Island.

When Godfrey was advanced in rank to colonel, Doane became a captain and continued under Godfrey's service. In June 1782, Doane was active in rescuing a brigantine and other smaller vessels when a British privateer attempted to seize and take them from Chatham harbor.[3]

*Near the close of the war the town became the scene of events more stirring perhaps than any that had occurred before during the struggle. On the 20th of June 1782 a British privateer daringly entered the harbor on the east side of the town and attempted to seize and carry away some of the shipping in the harbor. It appears that among the vessels at anchor within the harbor was a brigantine, called the* Joseph, *Peter Wells, master. The Captain and most of the crew…were spending the night on shore. About sunrise the next morning those living near the harbor discovered a British flag hoisted upon the brigantine.*

*A boat's crew from a British privateer outside the harbor had ventured in and seized the vessel, together with a schooner and sloop then in the harbor, and were intending to make off with them. An alarm gun was immediately sounded and a flag was hoisted on the hill opposite the harbor, that being used as the alarm post of the town.*

*Col. Benjamin Godfrey, Joseph Doane, Esq., Mr. Richard Sears, and a number of others assembled on the said hill armed. They were members of the local militia and proceeded at once to the beach opposite where the brigantine lay…In about the space of an hour after this, the brigantine and privateer as also the sloop (the schooner having grounded) got under way and were going out of the harbor, the privateer about half-a-mile ahead…As soon as they got underway, the said Godfrey, Doane and others to the number of 50 and upwards, assembled on the beach as*

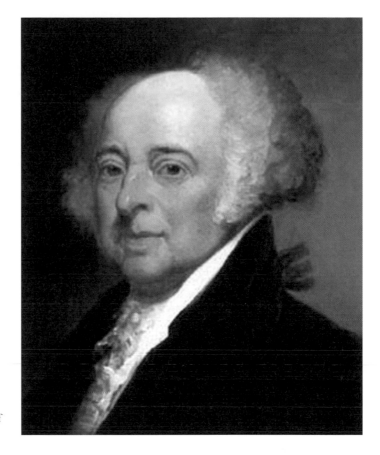

John Adams was Ansel Nickerson's defense attorney and successfully defended the young man—who was rescued by Captain Doane from the schooner *Abigail* against murder charges. Adams later became the second president of the United States.

*aforesaid, commenced and kept up a constant fire on the privateer till they got out of the harbor, the privateer returning their fire incessantly with cannon and swivels, as they were going out.*

*It appears that the brigantine ran aground on the flats and listed over to one side…they on board ceased firing and taking to their boats, ran out of the harbor and got on board the privateer…Doane and others ordered some of their people aboard the said brigantine…struck the English and hoisted the Continental colors…[They] pursued in boats the said sloop who was gone off, supposed for New York…with part of the said brigantine's cargo on board and retook her and brought her into the harbor. Capt. Doane ordered about 20 of his men to remain on board the brigantine and dismissed the rest with orders to appear again at the alarm post upon the firing of three cannon.*

That same day, the cannons were fired again. Captain Doane and his company engaged another privateer, which they captured and for which they received salvage money. These funds were much needed. As Smith notes, the fishing and coasting business was practically ruined by the war and British privateers. At the beginning of the Revolution in Chatham there were thirty vessels and two hundred men involved in the maritime industry. At the war's close, only four or five ships remained in the harbor, and many crewmen were captured or died in prison ships.

After the Revolution, Captain Doane remained involved in local and commonwealth affairs, serving as a representative in the Massachusetts legislature from 1788 to 1790. He married twice. His first wife, Mercy Ryder of Chatham, died of smallpox in 1766. There were no children from that union. His second wife, Abigail Gould of Harwich, however, bore eleven children.

Captain Doane died in 1801 and Abigail followed in 1820 at age seventy-five.

# JOSHUA ATKINS
## (1777–1844)
### *Lost His Ships to Pirates*

C aptain Joshua Atkins was the son of William and Lydia (Nickerson) Atkins. He was born in Chatham a year after America declared its independence from England. His early years parallel the founding of the United States, and his loyalty to his homeland was twice put to the test in later years. Geneva Agnes (Nickerson) Eldredge, a great-granddaughter of Captain Joshua Atkins, has written a lively account of her ancestor's life and times.[1]

> [He] *was a man who descended from the nobility of England, and upon whose walls in the old "Square Top" at North Chatham hung the coat of arms of the Atkins family, which corresponds with that one in the South Transcript of Westminster Abbey, London, England, over the Atkins Tablet there. A duplicate can also be found in Kitteringham, Norfolk, in the beautiful old church near the ancient Atkins Manor House, where Sir Robert Atkins, one of the Barons of the Exchequer under Charles I and Charles II was buried in 1669.*
>
> *We also find that through his great grandmother, Constance Hopkins, he inherited the staunchness of the Pilgrim Fathers of* Mayflower *fame, for her father, Stephen, was a passenger on that voyage, and the name of Stephen Hopkins is well known in Pilgrim history.*
>
> *With the refinement of his noble ancestors coupled with the integrity of his Pilgrim Fathers, Joshua must have been a young man of pleasing personality to the young ladies of his day.* [He was] *a well built young man and if he followed the Atkins traits, blue-eyed and light haired, frank and open faced, rather serious minded with a sense of honor higher than the average and a stern courage and strength in the faith of his honest convictions. But…he journeyed up to what was known as "Red River Country"* [now South Chatham] *to find the treasure of his heart.*

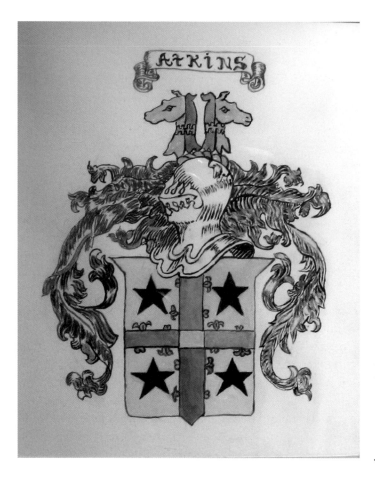

A modern adaptation of the Atkins family crest, the emblem that hung in Captain Atkins and Mehitable's treasured Square Top homestead in Chatham and the captain's ancestral home in England. *Joseph A. Nickerson Jr. Collection.*

*Like all men of his day "he went down to the sea in ships," for to them the planks of their vessel decks were far more familiar than the boards of their kitchen floors. And perhaps somewhere between trips, there was a party, or "spree" as they called it then, which he attended, and there met Mehitable, with her merry quip and ready jest drew him as a magnet and before he knew it his heart was lost…A fine example of the attraction of the opposite…A fine couple but so different, he with his quiet dignified manner, and she with her roguish eyes and ready smile.*

Before marrying Mehitable "Hittie" Eldredge in 1799, Captain Atkins sailed to Maine where he supervised the felling and cutting to size of the lumber intended for the home he would build for his bride-to-be. With the lumber safely loaded, he ran the British blockade—probably by flying a British flag—and made his way safely to Old Harbor in Chatham. There he built a beautiful, square-top house for Hittie.

Like many New England men in the late eighteenth century, Joshua turned to the sea at an early age and was master of the 147-ton brig *Sally* in 1796. A Boston marine list, dated September 1801, notes the arrival of the brig *Triton*, with Joshua Atkins as its master. Its port of departure was Lisbon and the voyage was made in forty-three days.

From Lisbon, the *Triton* was most likely to have had a hold full of salt, wine, oranges and possibly lace, needles and pins, too.

While that may have been a usual cargo, the trip itself was unusual. The report adds:

> *Capt. Atkins informs "Action fought in Mediterranean terminated in capture of 4 French sail—3 escaped…Alarm for six Spanish Ships of War. British went after them. British battleship* Hannibal *lost by getting ashore." Capt. Atkins informs he understood Peace considered to be concluded between Spain and Portugal.*

Another Boston marine list, also dated 1801, has Captain Atkins arriving from Boston at Norfolk on the schooner *Cameron*, and later arriving at Boston from Lisbon in a mere twenty-five days on the same vessel—a hitherto unmatched record time for that distance. Atkins is listed as master of the brig *Orion* in the same year. Its route was Havana to Boston.

Transatlantic voyages were not for the timid during this period. British naval personnel boarded American ships, sometimes forcing the crews into service for the Crown. Captain Atkins was captured three times by the British—twice he was sent ashore with his crew because he would not enlist in the British navy. He was fortunate that the punishments were so light—they could have meant imprisonment in addition to the capture of his vessel.

Nathaniel Eldredge, his father-in-law, had been taken prisoner by the British while fishing on Nantucket Shoals when Hittie was a small child. When offered his liberty if he would join the English, Nathaniel refused, saying he would rather rot in prison than fight against his country. He was confined in Dartmoor Prison for three years.

From the Kittredge Papers in the Barnstable Sturgis Library there is an account of the registry of the schooner *Liberty* of Chatham, with Joshua Atkins listed as master in 1807. The account notes that this vessel was used on foreign voyages. There were four owners listed—all Kendricks and all from Chatham. In 1809, Atkins was master of the *Pomona*, a 253-ton vessel owned by Boston investors.

Captain Atkins had a deep-water brig named *Morning Star*, which he sailed from Chatham to Demerara, West Indies, with a load of salt fish during the War of 1812. He arrived safely, sold his cargo and had an uneventful trip home until he reached the Nantucket Shoals. There he was boarded by English pirates who demanded that he give up all the money he had on board. Here is the account of the incident written by Captain Atkins's granddaughter:

> *But Capt. Atkins had no idea of passing that over without an argument, so he refused point blank, and explained that the money did not belong to him, but to poor men and some widows and orphans who would suffer from the need of it. Little cared the pirates for that, "Lash him to the mouth of the cannon," ordered their Captain, "and shoot when I give the order." The crew obeyed and for four hours Captain Joshua remained lashed there, while the pirates hunted every nook and corner of his vessel. Now and then they*

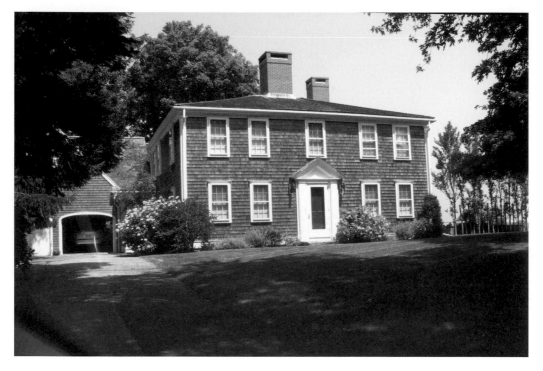

Square Top, as it appears today, is the house built by Captain Joshua Atkins for his wife Mehitable from lumber he brought from Maine around 1799. *Photo by Joseph A. Nickerson.*

*would ask him if he was ready to tell, and each time he answered "no," at last…the Pirate captain gave the order to fire but first he said "Captain Atkins, I give you one last chance before we shoot you, will you tell where the money is?"*

*"Sir, I shall never tell…," replied Captain Atkins, looking fearlessly into the eyes of the pirate captain. There were men at the cannon ready to fire, there was the helpless Cape Cod Captain lashed to its mouth, the pirate captain between the two…he shook his head and for a moment paused, then in clear commanding tones he gave the order, "Unlash him, he is too brave a man to die like that." So they set him adrift with two of his crew, retaining his vessel and the rest of his crew.*

There is another version of this part of the story where it says that Captain Atkins, who was a Mason, gave the Masonic distress sign that indicated trouble. The British pirate was also a Mason, and recognizing a fellow Mason, he set the captain free, declaring that Atkins was the bravest fellow he had ever met. Both versions have the happy ending that brought Captain Joshua back to his dear Hittie. His granddaughter Agnes provides the ending of the story:

*When Captain Joshua arrived home, with no ship, without crew, and with no other clothing beside that which he wore, he laid his bundle of few belongings on the table and with a voice shaken with pent up emotion said, "Hittie, here's all I've got left. The vessel and everything lost to English pirates," and tears streamed down his cheeks. Standing in the circle of his arms she looked into his face and said, "It will be easy to get another vessel, but Josh, I could never find another man like you."*

Captain Atkins continued to sail at least until 1827 when he took the *Caledonia* to Baltimore. When he gave up the sea, he established a fishing business with Caleb and Salathiel Nickerson of Chatham, built saltworks at the Old Harbor and tended to his substantial farm at Square Top.

Captain Atkins had been subject to fits of epilepsy for years, and he died during one such fit in 1844. He and his beloved Hittie are interred side by side in Union Cemetery, Chatham.

# BARZILLAH HARDING
## (1788–1855)
### Packet Captain for Thirty Years

Captain Harding's first name isn't a common one. Perhaps that's why records provide at least five different ways to spell it. We're going with Barzillah, but Barzilla, Barzillai, Barzila and Barsillah are all used in referring to this Chatham sea captain. In his time, spelling was by sound, and not everybody's "sound" spelling was alike, to be sure.

The good captain was a packet boat master. Packets are vessels, sometimes called "coasters." They plied the waters of the Atlantic Coast—in Harding's case primarily from Boston to New York, with an occasional stop in New Haven.

British privateers often accosted these vessels, trying to impress men they deemed to be English subjects. Proof of citizenship was found to be necessary. In our collection of materials on Captain Barzillah, there is an affidavit issued by the United States of America, No. 4121, which states:

> *I, Jeddiah Huntington, Collector of the district of New-London, hereby certify, that Barzilla* [sic] *Harding, an American seaman, aged nineteen years, or thereabouts, of the height of five feet eight inches of light complexion, has this day produced to me proof, in the manner directed in the act entitled "An act for the relief and protection of American seamen," and pursuant to the said act I do hereby certify that the said Barzilla* [sic] *Harding is a Citizen of the United States of America.*
>
> *Signed by Jeddiah Huntington, 5ᵗʰ of May, 1807.*

This was followed on April 1, 1811, with that well-known message, which begins, "Greetings: You, being appointed Sergeant of a Company in the third Brigade and fifth Division of the Militia of Massachusetts…" It is signed by Jonathan Snow, lieutenant colonel and commandant.

After serving his tour of duty, Barzillah returned to the sea. Early packet boats traveling to and from Boston afforded reliable sources for express and mail. According

James Bears received $250 from Barzilla [sic] Harding for removing the captain's vessel from where it had gone aground and taking it to the harbor on the point of Monomoy Island. *Courtesy of the Chatham (MA) Historical Society, Inc.*

to Simeon L. Deyo's *History of Barnstable County*, Barzillah Harding and Heman Smith were thus engaged prior to 1829.

There are many interesting papers in the Barzillah Harding archives: manifests, wharfing fees, bills of settlement, cargo lists, et cetera, all of which make fascinating reading. They are from several vessels, specifically sloop *Galen*, sloop *Canton* and the schooner *Two Friends*. One cargo in 1819, lists "1500 Quentails Dryed Codfish," unloaded in New Haven; from Newport, 815 bushels of corn put onboard the sloop *Galen*; another lists 63 barrels of turpentine and 75 barrels of clam bait; still another lists potatoes, pepper and ginger, a half-gross of hooks, oil [whale oil], vinegar, candles and wood.

The sloop *Canton* was a forty-six-ton sloop built in 1826. One manifest lists flint glass brought to Chatham by Captain Barzillah from Boston and given to the Chatham Congregational Church in 1831, when the church was located adjacent to Union Cemetery.

There is an instrument, dated March 12, 1836, regarding the enrollment of the *Canton*, issued:

> *In conforming to an Act of Congress of the United States, entitled "An Act for Enrolling and Licensing ships or vessels to be employed in the Coasting Trade and Fisheries, and for regulating same" naming Captain Barsillai [sic] Harding, together with five other owners as having satisfied the requirements, thus enrolling Sloop* Canton *as of the above date.*

Deyo's *History of Barnstable County* has the sloop *Canton* being run by Barzillah Harding for thirty years as a packet to Boston. The *Canton* is considered the first regular packet between Boston and Chatham from 1826 on. She had been built at the foot of Water Street in Chatham in 1826. Several Chatham residents owned an interest in her, as was customary in those and later times. According to Edwin F. Eldredge in his *Chatham Sea Captains*, the *Canton* did a good freighting business. There were many small vessels that would go over to Nantucket every year with produce for barter; others ran between Chatham, New Bedford, New York and intervening ports carrying fish and returning with flour, grain and the like.

Captain Barzillah Harding and his wife, the former Patty Bangs, were married April 12, 1839, and lived on Water Street, in what is now called the Old Village. They had eleven children. Barzillah and Patty are interred at the Union Cemetery in Chatham.

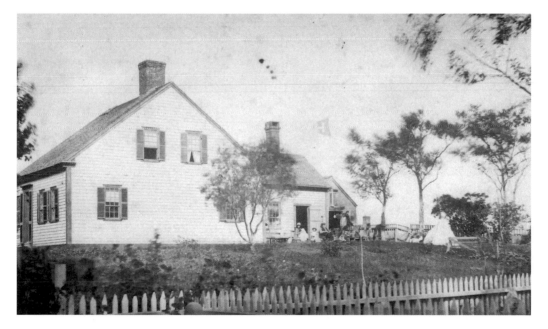

Captain Barzillah Harding's house, a full Cape, was located on Water Street in the Old Village. This photo was taken circa 1860. *Joseph A. Nickerson Jr. Collection.*

*Part II*

# The Nineteenth-Century Masters

# JUSTUS DOANE
## (1807–1853)
### *Great Race to California*

Four clipper ships were involved in the 1852–1853 "Great Race to California," sailing from New York to San Francisco. Both Kittredge in his 1935 volume, *Shipmasters of Cape Cod*, and Howe and Matthews's *American Clipper Ships*, provide accounts of the race. The ships involved were the *John Gilpin* with Justus Doane as captain; the *Flying Fish*, skippered by Captain Nickels; the *Wild Pigeon*, with Captain Putnam as master; and the *Trade Wind*, with Captain Webber as master.

The facts are that the *Flying Fish* made the course in 92 days and 4 hours, arriving on January 1, preceded by the *Gilpin*, which arrived the day before, but took 93 days and 20 hours to make the voyage. The *Pigeon* took 118 days and the *Trade Wind* was last, having had a fire that burned for 8 hours on the way. Following is our favorite version of the race of the clipper ships, written by Kittredge:

> *Captain Justus Doane, of Chatham, got into such a race in 1852–53—one of the most thrilling contests in the annals of the sea. Doane had already made a place for himself in the front rank of Clipper Captains by his performance in the R.B. Forbes which he had taken on her maiden voyage 'round the world the year before. On the first lap he had hung up a new record for merchantmen by reaching Honolulu from Boston in 96 days, 12 hours—land to land. He followed this by a run of 21 days, 13 hours to Hong Kong for the second leg of the voyage—remarkable time and close to the record (and he wound up by beating the Sea Witch home from Whampoa [Hong Kong] by 6 days). Any one of the three sections of this voyage would have done him credit; taken in combination, they placed Capt. Doane close to the top of his profession. He got home in July, 1852, took the summer off, and in October was ready to go to sea again, this time in command of Samuel Hall's new medium clipper, the John Gilpin.*

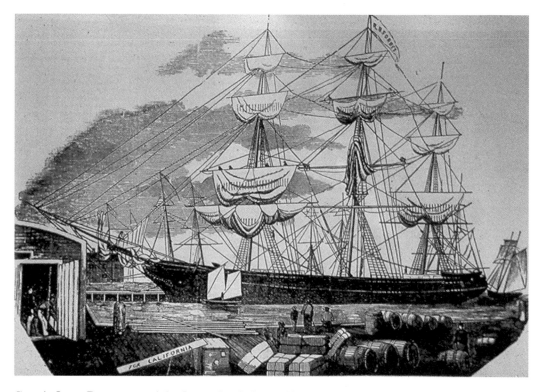

Captain Justus Doane entered the first ranks of clipper ship captains by sailing the *R.B. Forbes* from Boston to Honolulu in 96 days and 12 hours, land to land. *Joseph A. Nickerson Jr. Collection.*

*He left New York in her on her maiden voyage (October 27), bound for California; 2 days behind him came Captain Nickels in Donald McKay's new extreme Clipper,* Flying Fish, *one third larger than the* Gilpin *and much sharper in design.*

The question was whether Doane could hold his lead against such a competitor and reach San Francisco before him. Two days was not much of a margin over a course where anything under 110 days was called unusual, and when the record—made only three times in the history of sail—was 89 days. But Captain Doane did not intend to be overtaken if he could help it.

At the equator, Nickels had caught up, but because he thought that he was wiser than the sailing directions and tried to cut corners, he found himself too far to the westward and wasted precious time in clearing Cape St. Roque, the eastern tip of Brazil. While Nickels was thus trying to beat the doldrums, Doane was flying south as fast as driving winds could carry him, and off the Horn he was a day ahead.

*But here the* Flying Fish *showed her quality. Her great size and weight and her enormously heavy spars carried her to the westward even in the teeth of the gales, and she came up with and passed the little* Gilpin, *which in spite of everything that Doane could crowd on her, was no match for the terrific head seas that swept her from stem to stern. Nickels, so the story goes, invited Doane to dine with him on board as he roared past. Doane's reply—fortunately, perhaps—is not recorded.*

*Until they reached the Equator, Nickels held his one day lead; then Doane and his vessel hit their stride: the* Gilpin *came up with the* Flying Fish, *passed her, and sailed into San Francisco one day ahead, after a passage of 93 days, 20 hours. Nickels, who came in the next day, had, to be sure, made it in 92 days, 4 hours, but Doane was content. And well he may have been, for on the merit of sheer seamanship he had easily surpassed his rival, having outwitted him at the Equator, having taken only two days longer to get by Cape Horn, and having passed him on the Equator headed North—all in a smaller and fuller-modeled ship.*

A footnote from Kittredge: "After this great race Captain Doane retired and went home to Chatham, where he intended to pass the rest of his life in peace." Captain Justus Doane and his wife, Keziah Nye, also a Chathamite, lived in a hip roof, two-family house on Main Street, at or near the site of the present Pate's Restaurant. The house was torn down in the 1930s. The couple had no children.

Captain Doane finally consented, reluctantly, to make one more voyage. With his wife he sailed to Calcutta where Mrs. Doane died of cholera. The captain succumbed to "brain fever" one day later. Both were buried there in 1853.

# HIRAM HARDING
## (1814–1878)
### *African Misadventure*

Young Hiram went to sea when he was just eleven years old, shipping as a cook on the Grand Banks schooner *Sally & Betsy* bound for Labrador in the summer of 1826. He must have been a passable cook because he went on at least two other schooners in that same capacity: the *Caledonia* with Captain Joshua Atkins on a trip to Baltimore, then to Alexandria on the *Pioneer*.

Our captain-to-be gave up cooking in 1828, and went to sea as an ordinary seaman on the brig *Mohawk*. Between voyages, Hiram spent a few weeks going to school, crowding school learning in between sea learning. Sometimes he stayed on shore as long as several months, always squeezing schooling into his life. That pattern was followed by a few of his peers. In Hiram's case, he wanted to rise from an ordinary seaman to become what he dreamed of being: a master mariner. That required schooling!

By 1830, Hiram sailed aboard a new vessel, the brig *Sylph*, as a full-fledged second mate. That same year he also served as second mate aboard the brig *Cervantes*, and the ship *Seaman*. Second Mate Hiram made his first foreign voyage in the square-rigger, the brig *Casket*, bound for Palermo and Malta with Captain Mark Snow in 1830. By the tender age of seventeen, Hiram was promoted to first mate, sailing on the brig *Palm*.

In 1835, at age twenty-one, he became a full-fledged captain in command of a new vessel, the brig *Pearl*. He continued in command of her for twelve years, running regularly on "the line" between Boston and Philadelphia, carrying freight and passengers, winter and summer.

There followed a succession of craft Captain Hiram had built: the barks *Sterling*, *Harvester* and *Cambridge*. In these vessels he voyaged to all parts of the world—England, France, Sicily, Amsterdam, Turkey, the East and West Indies, Australia, East Africa, Russia and San Francisco. He commanded vessels for thirty-nine years, retiring in 1875 following the loss of the bark *Harvester*. The accident took place on the coast of Africa. Here is the captain's story of the loss in his own words:

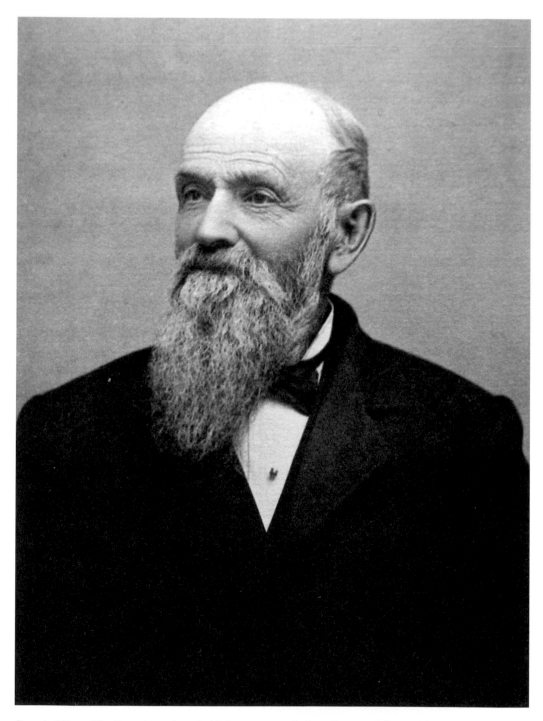

Captain Hiram Harding, shown here in his later years, sailed to all parts of the world. He was master for thirty-nine years, retiring in 1875. *Joseph A. Nickerson Jr. Collection.*

*When daylight came we found ourselves cast away on the coast of a veritable desert. We were sighted by the native Africans who paddled alongside in canoes and climbed aboard, their numbers constantly increasing as they swarmed to the coast on camels from the interior.*

*They were terrible looking fellows and it was threatening to our lives as they took possessions, destroyed or took our stock while looking for specie [gold]. In spite of the seriousness of the situation, I was compelled to laugh outright at the ridiculous picture presented by the big chief one day when he dressed himself up in my plug hat and frock coat and, after hopped around in a war dance. Demanded the treasure they were certain was hidden aboard. They went ashore at sunset each day, remaining all night and dancing like devils around their campfire.*

*The first night my chief mate deserted with several men declaring they would not stay and be murdered.*

*Next night I sent away the second mate with some men to make for some port and assistance.*

*I stuck by the ship and the $20,000 in specie with 4 men, one being young Walter Eldredge, a Chatham boy, now Master of one of the Baltimore Steamers. He showed the stuff he was made of at this time by saving the lives of all of us. The next night, when realizing the growing ferocity of the natives toward us, I felt that to avoid being murdered we too must abandon the ship.*

*As soon as the black devils went ashore at dark we loaded our remaining boat with what provisions had not been destroyed, my chronometer and other articles and stowed in also the 20 bags containing the $20,000.*

*When all was ready to lower the boat from the davits a heavy sea swept in causing the ship to roll, and away went the boat from her fastenings down into the water, bottom up, dumping all our goods and treasure into the sea. The boat began to drift away, and I said "There goes our only hope for safety" when young Eldredge plunged overboard and swam to the boat. We threw our oars toward him, one of which he secured, and paddled the boat alongside, thus saving our lives, which was all we now had left worth fighting for.*

*With what little provisions we could now throw into the boat, we left the doomed* Bark *and started on the long pull across the Gulf of Aden [south entrance to the Red Sea] toward the port of that name, which we reached after 3 days in the open boat, entirely exhausted. There I engaged a steamer with divers and wrecking crew armed sufficiently to stand off any black devils who might dispute our authority and returned to the* Bark, *hoping to be able to recover the specie, but it had all become buried in the shifting sands. The vessel also had been practically destroyed by the natives so we returned without saving anything.*

Captain Harding was sixty-nine years of age and, after such an experience, it is not surprising that he would choose to come home and leave seagoing to younger men. The handsome house, which Captain Hiram built in 1839, still stands on Old Harbor Road. Now an inn, it is appropriately known as "The Captain's House." Its lumber was

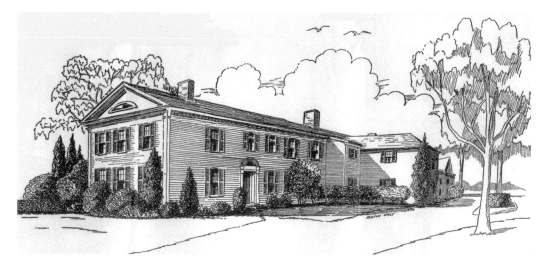

Captain Hiram Harding's beautiful house on Old Harbor Road in Chatham was built in 1839. Today it welcomes visitors as The Captain's House guesthouse. *Drawing by Milton Welt.*

shipped from Maine via schooners, which discharged their cargo in what is now known as the Cow Yard. At that time, large vessels could easily navigate the harbor there.

Captain Hiram Harding was an influential man in Chatham, carrying on a dizzying list of landlubber activities after his retirement. He was a notary, a justice of the peace, a wreck commissioner, a director of the Barnstable County Fire Insurance Co., a prominent member of the Chatham ME Church and for thirty-five years, an influential member of the Boston Marine Society.[1]

Captain Hiram and his wife, Lydia Gould, were parents of eight children. Mrs. Harding died in 1873. Their daughter Marianne is the only one of their children who lived longer than the captain. Captain Harding and his family are interred in Seaside Cemetery.

# ELIJAH CROSBY
## (1819–1898)
### *Savior of the Shipwrecked*

Captain Elijah Crosby was one of those far traveling, old Chatham sea captains that people want to know more about, said an old, circa 1947 Boston newspaper clipping that can be found in the Chatham Historical Society's archives. It notes that during his sailing days, the captain often took his wife along on long voyages, and sometimes his children, Cora and Arthur, too. Following is an extract from a newspaper article in which the captain's daughter Cora C. Meads was interviewed about what she remembers and was told of her father's days at sea:

*She is in her 87th year and she had been 'round the Horn with her father, her mother and little brother in those rugged days of iron men and wooden ships.*

*They were 104 days out of Boston, going to Valparaiso, and 102 days homebound for New York in the bark* Schamyl *of Boston in the year 1862. "We went 'round the Horn and it was like a mill-pond—father flew a kite for my little brother (Arthur)."*

*"I was just two years old," she said, "but I remember what they told me. I had my second birthday at Valparaiso. It was some days before we arrived there that the men were found adrift. Mother saw a speck on the ocean. She called the mate and he got the spyglass. Then father came up and looked through it. 'Looks to me like a signal of distress,' he said. Finally we reached them. There were 12 men in an open boat. One lay in the bottom of the boat. The men dropped him over the side of their boat before they came aboard our bark. They were very bad off, because they had been without food and water a long time. Later, the Captain who was with them said they had been adrift 30 days. Something had happened to their ship; I don't know what it was. They had gone ashore on an island, but they didn't stay long. 'Better to drown or starve than be eaten by Cannibals,' the Captain said. His name was Wood.*

*"Father had to ration them. One man got into the hard bread—pilot crackers I guess you'd call them now. One had to have both legs amputated. They were in awful shape.*

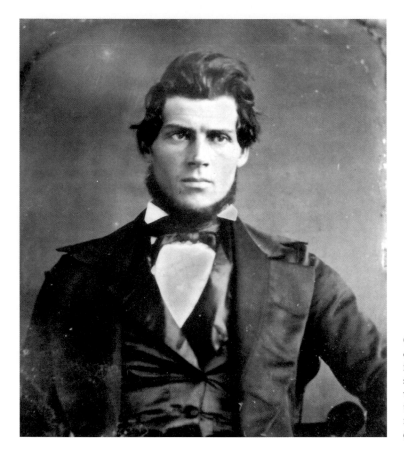

Captain Elijah Crosby,
circa 1845, "one of those
far traveling, old Chatham
sea captains that people
want to know," around the
time he became a master
mariner. *Photograph courtesy
of his grandson, Jeff Eldredge.*

*They had frozen fingers and mother had to tear up my nightgown to make bandages.
Captain Wood couldn't eat supper; he was so overcome. He stayed on deck, with his head
on the rail.*

*"'What can I do to repay you for your kindness?' he asked father. Father said he
wanted nothing. Captain Wood said 'Your kindness will not go unrewarded.' He formed
a devotion for father and, afterward, they corresponded for years. I remember going to the
post office—'Oh, a letter from Captain Wood,' mother would say. He was a big man.
Mother gave him some of father's clothes and put father's necktie on him. Captain Wood
said, 'How do I look for a castaway?' He told father that the way he kept alive was by
thumping the rest of the men in the boat. He'd give them a punch and say, 'Brace up
there.' That seemed to give him and the others new strength.*

*"There were some things in the boat. He gave mother a dozen spoons and two
nutcrackers. But, right after we arrived in Valparaiso, Captain Wood went to the British
consulate. Some time later father received a beautiful chronometer watch from London,
inscribed with details of the rescue inside. You could run the ship by it, father said. It was
a gift from the British government in gratitude for saving the English crew.*

*"Mother gave the watch to my brother, Arthur. Now his son, Arthur P. Crosby of
Brookline, has it. I believe it's in a safe deposit box in Boston."*

*Mrs. Meads then brought out a stout old photo album. She showed a picture of Captain Wood that had been sent from England to her father. We were taken through rooms of the old house and shown great oil paintings of the barks, the* Schamyl, *the* Stillman B. Allen, *and the* Chester...*And, the figures of the crews and general detail seemed to be worked out with a fine eye to authenticity...*

*"On the return voyage from Valparaiso, the* Schamyl *brought a heavy load of copper ore and wool." Mrs. Meads continued, "Mother said, when she went aboard, there was only one plank between her and eternity. The deck was so close to the sea..."*

*We questioned her more about Captain Crosby. Mrs. Meads concluded with this episode: Her father came up to a crowd gathered at a ferry slip in Chelsea. A woman had fallen overboard. There were just exclamations, no one was doing anything about it. "Sling a pole down there," Captain Crosby called out, "and I'll get her out." He saved the woman. His hand was severely injured. He went away. Some weeks later, on his return, he was in a ship chandler's shop and the proprietor inquired about his injured hand. "Oh, I got this hauling out a woman who was drowning," said Captain Crosby. He was told then that there had been an advertisement in the papers—relatives were trying to locate the rescuer. Captain Crosby went to them.*

*At this point Mrs. Meads brought out a silver cup. There is an inscription on it which reads: To Captain Elijah Crosby from Mrs. Jon Loring of Chelsea as a token of gratitude and respect for his praiseworthy effort in saving her life at the Chelsea Ferry Landing, July 8, 1855.*

*Captain Crosby's daughter finished her account "He was quite impulsive in his actions. He was fearless."*

How did this fearless captain's career on the sea begin? On his first voyage, at age ten, Elijah Crosby was the cook for wages of three dollars a month on a fishing schooner carrying a crew of ten men. Captain Crosby became a master at age twenty-six. He worked successfully as a master mariner for another twenty-six years until 1871. He was master of three barks, the *Chester*, the *Lamplighter* and the *Schamyl*. He was never shipwrecked.

Captain Elijah's first vessel, the bark *Chester*, had a crew list at one juncture that provides wages and personal information:

*Crosby, Master: Joshua W. Eldredge, Mate 18 yrs., 5 ft. 6½ ins., light comp., brown hair, wages $30 mo.: John Young, 2nd Mate, 30 yrs., 5 ft. 3 ins., light comp., brown hair, $25 mo.: B.F. Patterson, cook/steward, 30 yrs., 5 ft. 3 ins., ruddy comp., brown hair, wages $28 mo.*[1]

There is a log of the *Chester*, dating from July 14, 1851, through May 12, 1853, which is a treasure beyond words. It is not exactly clear who kept this log—probably several men at different times—but they have in common unique spelling and provide vivid descriptions of the workings of a very large vessel. The following entries offer an example:

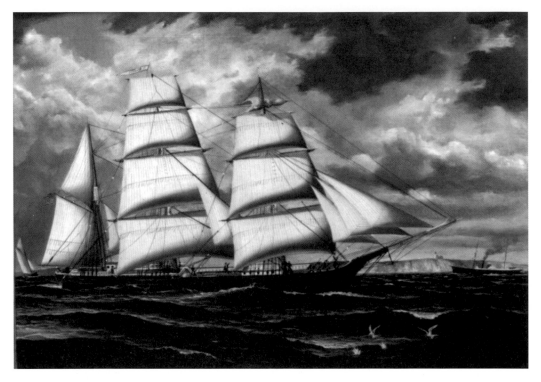

The bark *Schamyl*, outbound from the Mediterranean in 1864. The *Schamyl* was one of three barks commanded by Capain Elijah Crosby during his career. *Courtesy of the Chatham (MA) Historical Society, Inc.*

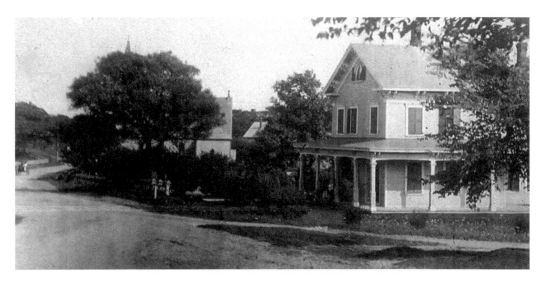

Captain Elijah Crosby's house was located on the corner of Main Street and Stage Harbor Road where a bank now stands on the rotary built years after his death. *Joseph A. Nickerson Jr. Collection.*

*Monday, October 3, 1851: At 1 pm a squall from S.W., took in light sails and dubled reafed the topsails. At 3 set topgallant sails over single reafed topsails. At 6 tuck in topgallant sails. Middle part fresh gails from N W and raney. At 2 am tuck in mainsail and outer jib. Latter part heavey gailes and passing clouds. At 9 closed reafed the topsails. At noon wore[2] ship to the northward.*

*Saturday, February 14, 1852: Commences with a fresh and clowday with all sails set. 3 pm Sancicty Head bore W S W 16 miles from which I take my departure from. 4 pm increasing breese and clowday with snow at times. Took in royal and flying gib and gaft topsails, staysails and topgallant sails. With heavy swell on, 6 pm duble reaft the topsail and stowed the outer gib. 9 calm with thick snow. Midknight took in misen spanker increasing breese with a sea on. 4 am reefs out of each topsail and set gib...*

There are many scheduled trips back and forth from Boston to New York and Philadelphia documented in this log. The ships carried coal and iron for Boston, and, in one entry, on the fifth trip to Philadelphia, they unloaded and "tow[ed] down to Richmond" to load coal and tow back to Philadelphia. There they unloaded again to take on deck a load of 500 barrels of sweet potatoes, besides 260 tons of coal in her hold—thence to Boston. On the way back to Boston the wind increased to a gale and

*at 2 a.m., a sea came aboard the starboard bow...and at 3:20 shipped a sea over the deck and washed several barrels of sweet potatoes overboard. The next morning...at 8, took another sea over the deck which "stove in" 3 barrels of potatoes and washed over at least two more barrels. The rest of those potatoes were secured and landed safely in Boston.*

On another trip from Boston to Mobile in January, the bark *Chester* carried a load of ice. The trip was made in twenty-two days—"All of this day fine and pleasant weather. The stevedores finished discharging the ice, the Captain discharged the second mate. So ends this day."

There followed another trip back to New York via Philadelphia with bales of cotton—125 earmarked for Philadelphia, over 700 for New York. And so it went, through every imaginable variety of weather.

Captain Crosby went back and forth for more than twenty years. Interspersed with trips on the *Chester* were voyages on the bark *Schamyl*—one to Oporto, Portugal, in 1863. The vessel was carrying 1,540 barrels of flour and 13,928 bushels of wheat from Boston. On that trip, the *Schamyl* went from London to Lisbon with 37,800 barrel staves and "291,400 of same."

To illustrate what cargo might be typical and also how much money each variety might bring, when sold, we have a record of a trip from New York to Cadiz in 1864 where the cargo included:

> *60 barrels resin @ $1.25*
> *69 barrels of beef and lard @ $1.25*
> *20 cases bacon @ $1.75 case*
> *20,000 light pipe staves @ $39/m*
> *3 cases books*
> *100 barrels refined petro*
> *10,000 barrel staves*
> *and another 40,000 light pipe staves.*

A fairly typical export from the Mediterranean area, such as this cargo from Messina, Sicily, in 1866, included casks of olive oil, canary seed (!), casks of wine, assorted nutmeats, lemons and oranges in great quantity, all bound for Boston.

Through the kindness and resourcefulness of Captain Elijah's great granddaughter, Priscilla Crosby Hickman, we have a copy of a list of Lloyd's of London reporting all the voyages that the captain made in the barks while the vessels were insured by Lloyd's.[3]

According to Edwin F. Eldredge in his unpublished manuscript, *Sea Captains of Chatham*, after he retired from the sea, Captain Elijah Crosby first went into the coal business, and later the lumber business. When he died in 1898, he was buried in Chatham's Seaside Cemetery.

# DAVID H. CROWELL
## (1820–1920)
### *Gold Rush and Civil War Memories*

With the outbreak of the Civil War, Captain David H. Crowell enlisted in the U.S. Navy at forty-one years of age, after decades at sea. He was immediately assigned to the sloop USS *Tuscarora*, which was commissioned December 5, 1861, at Philadelphia. Built by Merrick & Sons, it displaced 1,457 tons, was over 198 feet long and had a speed of eleven knots. Commander Tunis A.M. Craven was in command.

> *Captain David H. Crowell of Chatham has been appointed Acting Master in the United States Navy. He has accepted the appointment and reported himself to the Commodore at the Brooklyn Navy Yard. He has orders, we learn, to join the sloop-of-war* Tuscarora, *at Philadelphia. Captain Crowell is in every respect worthy of the honor conferred upon him.*[1]

The *Tuscarora* sailed for Southampton, England, under orders to capture or sink the Confederate cruiser CSS *Nashville*, which was the first vessel to show the Confederate flag in English waters. Sealed orders directed the ship to bring the American ambassador back to the U.S. in the event England should enter the war as an ally of the Confederacy. With sentiment in England favoring the Confederacy, Craven was unable to pursue the *Nashville* when it left for Gibraltar. The *Tuscarora*'s tour of duty in European waters ended when it was assigned blockade duty off the United States coast, in the event of an attack on the nation's capital. Illness forced Captain Crowell to retire from the navy.

Before the Civil War, however, the California gold rush of 1849 was a pivotal event to many Americans. In response to gold being discovered, Captain Crowell became a founding member of the Chatham Trading and Mining Co., a group of young men who drew up formal articles of agreement in Boston on July 10, 1849. The members of this company read like the founding members of Chatham! As such, they warrant

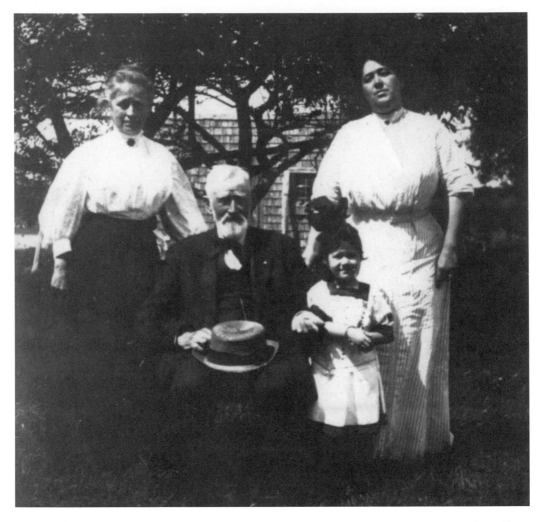

Captain David H. Crowell, *seated*, is photographed around 1910 with, *from left*, daughter Mary Crowell Farmer, great-granddaughter Virginia Harding and granddaughter Edith Farmer Harding. *Courtesy of the Chatham (MA) Historical Society, Inc.*

enumerating: Elisha E. Atkins, David H. Crowell, Kimball R. Howes Jr., Alvah Ryder, Stephen V. Smith, Mark H. Crowell, Samuel P. Newcomb, Richard Smith, Reuben A. Snow, John Crowell and John Quinn. All were copartners in the Trading and Mining Expedition to California, as it was called.

Each member was given a cash sum of not more than $250 to be invested in provisions, cargo, implements and a house in California for the company. All parties were to refrain from any speculation or other business to the detriment of said company. All officers and seamen were to be chosen from the company; but, if deemed wise, a cook and steward might be shipped for the voyage.

The brig *William Penn* was the vessel chosen. There was a committee of three authorized to sell her whenever it deemed such sale was for the mutual interest of the owners. Captain David H. Crowell was to be the master, president and treasurer—to receive 2 percent upon sale of the net stock of the company for his services. Elisha Atkins was to be the secretary, Thatcher Ryder Jr. (David's father-in-law) was to purchase the necessary outfits for the voyage and John Quinn was to become a member of the company on arrival in California as per agreement.

From a news clip given to Edwin Eldredge—the author of two unpublished volumes entitled *Chatham Sea Captains* written in 1943—comes this report:

> When the gold sickness sent the '49ers westward, and men were washing the sands of California in search of the yellow metal (which all too many of them later spent in pleasures that turned out only mockeries in the end), Capt. Crowell carried a party of gold-seekers in the **William Penn** from Boston 'round the Horn to California. When the brig was [a few] days out it was dismantled in a hurricane on the southern edge of the Gulf Stream and capsized.
>
> In speaking of his experiences on this memorable trip, Capt. Crowell says: "We left Boston on July 28, 1849, carrying a cargo of building materials and seven passengers, with a crew numbering 10 men. On the 4th of August, when we were on the southern edge of the Gulf Stream, we were struck by a violent hurricane, which lasted but a short time, but threw the vessel on her beam-ends. The storm quickly passed. The topmasts and rigging were cut away and the vessel righted. After making temporary repairs we returned to Boston and made ready for a second trip."
>
> This vessel made its first start on July 28. Its second and successful attempt was made in the latter part of August, and the *Penn* reached California in 154 uneventful days. Not one of the men who were capsized that fourth day out on the *Penn* ever panned sufficient gold to be wealthy.

The brig stayed in Sacramento City about six months. While Captain Crowell never struck gold, he opened a shipboard bakery and sold cookies to the miners for eighty cents a dozen. Prices there were extravagantly high—flour was quoted at that time to be twenty-four cents a pound and everything else was proportionately expensive. Captain Crowell stayed on in California, largely to look after the owner's interests in the vessel. She was finally sold and Crowell, employed by the new owners, took the *Penn* on a seven-month trading voyage to the Sandwich Islands and Panama. When he returned he found the owners had failed, owing him fourteen hundred dollars. The only return he ever received was many years later when the man who had bought the *Penn* paid him a hundred dollars!

Captain Crowell made a second voyage to California in 1851 in command of the bark *J.J. Cobb*. There were thirty passengers—women and children—going to the Golden Gate to rejoin their husbands and fathers. The trip, with smooth seas and fair winds, made record time of only 130 days. The captain came back to Boston by way of Callao, Peru, the Chinchi Islands (probably to bring on a cargo of guano) and Baltimore, trading from port to port as he headed back to Massachusetts.

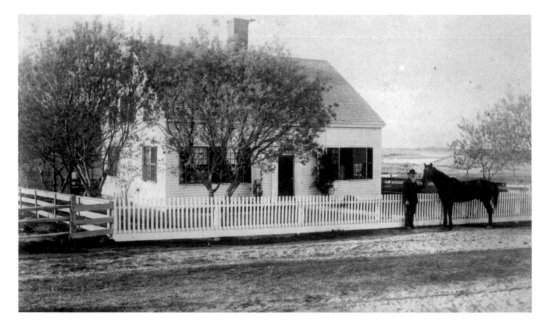

Captain David H. Crowell with his horse Charley, *at right*, in front of his home near Ryder's Cove in Chatham, Massachusetts. *Courtesy of the Chatham (MA) Historical Society, Inc.*

Captain Crowell had married Mercy Ryder in 1845. She accompanied him on many of his voyages. They had five children, of whom little is known except for two daughters: Mary, who married John Farmer, and Geneva, who married Frank Howes of New Bedford.

When asked by a visitor if he had not enjoyed his long years at sea, Captain Crowell responded, "Yes, but when she's on her beams' end and dips her yards under, it's then you think of home." At home, he became Chatham's superintendent of schools and was credited with "indefatigable exertion in building up our schools," according to the local newspaper. The good captain also was the Chathamport postmaster in 1903, keeping the mail in the cupboard beside his dining room fireplace. He died in 1920, just short of his hundredth birthday. He was eulogized as a prominent and substantial citizen on his death. Captain Crowell is buried in Chatham's Union Cemetery with his wife Mercy.

# GEORGE ELDRIDGE
## (1821–1900)
### *Hydrographer/Cartographer*

There is a tale illustrating "Chart George's" reputation as a navigator and sea captain. There was a bad northeasterly storm raging. A fleet of vessels had sought refuge in Plymouth Harbor and had been there for a couple of days. It was night, and out of the wild storm a vessel appeared, like a ghostly apparition. Someone asked what ship could it be that had survived the storm outside and proceeded now unharmed to anchorage? The reply was, "It could be no one but George Eldridge!"

It was 1849 when Captain Eldridge began making charts with his small son George Washington as his assistant. Their first charts were of waters off Chatham, then known to all mariners as the most dangerous part of the American coastline. The elder Eldridge's first completed chart included such forbidding places as Pollock Rip and the sandbars from Stone Horse to Handkerchief Shoal.

In December 1850 a violent storm with gale winds threw him from the mainmast to the deck of his coasting schooner, *Conway*. The fall left him with a permanent disability and a stoop. A severe storm several months after the captain's own accident created dangerous shoal conditions off Chatham. In April 1851 an inlet was opened, caused by the furious storm waves that pounded Nauset Beach. Those waves roiled seaward and caused a large quantity of sand to form dangerous shoals—Chatham New Harbor Bars—which were in the direct track of vessels. Although a buoy was placed off the bars, at night there were neither lights nor other marks to warn vessels of the danger. To that end, the captain worked feverishly to create a chart to mark this major danger.

He had taught himself surveying, starting out bravely to earn money for his family's support by preparing charts for other mariners. To do so, he accomplished something never before attempted in America—making a triangulation chart—plus he was on his way to becoming a renowned hydrographer and cartographer.

His reputation and his charts' accuracy were such that the U.S. government hired him to make its charts. In 1854, Captain Eldridge was given the position of

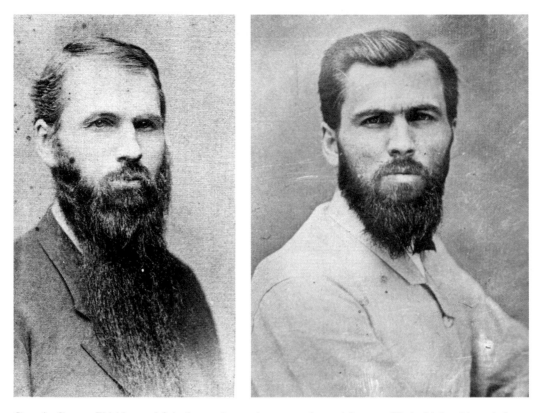

Captain George Eldridge, *at left*, hydrographer and cartographer, made maps filled with local knowledge. His son, George Washington Eldridge, *at right*, moved to Martha's Vineyard and created a tide book. *From* The Captain's Daughters of Martha's Vineyard *by Eliot Eldridge Macy.*

commander's counselor on the USS *Bibb*, under Lieutenant Commander Henry S. Stellwagen. During 1854 and 1855, Stellwagen, on loan to the U.S. Coast Survey, and Eldridge worked on mapping the full length and breadth of the bank most fishermen had called Middle Ground. On October 22, 1854, Stellwagen wrote to his superior:

> *I consider I have made an important discovery in the location of a 15 fathom bank lying in a line between Cape Cod and Cape Ann—with 40 and 50 fathoms inside and to northward of it and 35 fathoms just outside it. It is not on any chart I have been able to procure. We have traced nearly five miles in width and over six miles in length, it no doubt extending much further.*

Alexander Bache, the superintendent of the Coast Survey, noted in his annual report the significance of this discovery, "I propose to call this, from the name of its discoverer, Stellwagen's Bank." Eldridge served in that surveying/chart-making position for three years, after which he returned to Chatham and his own chart-making business. That was the beginning of a family business that is now a marine tradition. According to the Huntington Chart Collection records in the Maryland State Archives, he may have had some private sources of information in addition to his local knowledge. Records from the Huntington Collection note:

> *The Eldridge charts were not subsidized and were more expensive, but that they survived* [is] *because of good design, simplicity, omission of extraneous shore topography, legible sounds and notes, and the use of compass courses only. Eldridge's first chart, according to Guthorn,*[1] *was published in December 1851, while he was convalescing at home from an injury. Beginning in 1865, his charts were published by Samuel Thaxter & Son of Boston and were all lithographed.*

Peter Guthorn also noted that George Eldridge and his successors "introduce a new 'user friendliness' and concern for the fleet which was still largely sail through World War I." In 1854, Captain Eldridge published *Eldridge's Pilot for Vineyard Sound and Monomoy Shoals.* Its thirty-two pages were devoted to "dangers" and were rich with personal observations, compass courses and distances. In 1870, he published another book called *The Compass Test.*

Since he was ten years of age, young George W. Eldridge had been his father's close and increasingly valuable assistant. In 1870, the captain asked his son to move to Martha's Vineyard and sell the book and the charts. George W. sold both from a catboat, going out to the schooners in port. According to Robert Eldridge White Jr. and Linda Foster White's history of the family firm:

> [George W.] *was constantly asked by mariners what time the current turned to run East or West in the Sound. He then began making observations, and one day, while in the ship chandlery of Charles Holmes, made the first draft of a current table. Shortly after, with the help of his father, he worked out the tables for places other than Vineyard Sound, and in 1875 the first Tide Book was published. It did not take long for mariners to realize the value of this information, and it soon became an indispensable book to all who sailed the Atlantic Coast from New York east.*

In 1892 when his father was seventy, Captain George W. took over responsibility for making the charts. Those later charts carry the *W*, whereas the first charts were authored simply George Eldridge. Publishing *The Eldridge Tide and Pilot Book* is still a family business today. The book is printed annually. In 1910, Captain George W. Eldridge gave the actual management of the book over to family members as he wished to concentrate on the chart business and inventing aids to navigation.

In 1979, Robert Eldridge White, then the publisher, described additions made to the tide book:

> *Since the Captain's day there have been many changes and additions in the book to keep abreast of modern navigational aids. However, the Captain's policy of large type for*

*legibility in reading the tables, and his personal notes on tidal currents are regarded to be as important to the book as in the 1st year of publication.*

One of the captain's grandchildren recalls seeing her grandfather only once when the family came over from Vineyard Haven. She remembers him as a big man, with very broad shoulders but with his head slightly sunk between his shoulders because of the earlier injury. He had a full head of iron-gray hair and very deep black eyes beneath heavy brows. She added, also, that his wife, Eliza, was very self-centered. She took to her bed at age forty and stayed in bed for the next forty-one years until her death.

The captain was very fond of music. He played the violin well, and although he was not exactly a devout churchgoer, he attended services at the Baptist Church because it was an opportunity to play his violin. Captain George and his wife had four boys and a girl. George W. was the eldest. Son Hiram inherited his father's musical inclinations and became a composer of sorts. He owned a fine store in Buffalo, New York, that sold musical merchandise.

Captain Eldridge lived on Old Harbor Road, Chatham, across from the Congregational Church. A contemporary is quoted as saying that he had long white whiskers and always had a small, curly haired dog on a leash. The man who bought the captain's house found in a back room a lot of sheet music that had been composed by the captain. Eldridge made many of his charts in the back chamber, too. When the floors were replaced, the boards were almost worn through opposite a table used by Captain Eldridge and his assistant Mark Harding when making the charts. Harding did most of the lettering on the charts and was a fine penman.

Captain George Eldridge died in 1900 and is buried in Chatham's Seaside Cemetery. His son, George W. Eldridge, died in 1914 and is buried in Vineyard Haven.

# JOHN PAYNE
## (1821–1864)
### Lost at Sea with Family

There is a long, long list of vessels to which John Payne is connected, beginning as early as 1841. That would make him twenty years old at the outset of these records, but there is no indication of his status, whether he was mate or master at that time. The earliest entry in 1841 puts him on the *Monsoon* for the Packet Line going between Boston and New Orleans. During 1844, he is listed as being on both the schooner *Commodore Kearny* and the packet *Huron*. On the latter, he sailed for the Taylor & Merrill Line. The *Monsoon* and the *Huron* account for his sailing activity until 1848. These packets sailed most often between Boston, Savannah and New Orleans.

John Payne married Reliance W. Harding when he was twenty-five years old. His bride, then aged eighteen, was the daughter of James and Rebecca (Nickerson) Harding. Their first son, John, died when he was only a toddler, and a daughter, Rebecca, died as an infant. However, the couple was blessed with Madelia, born in 1848, Emma in 1857, Lizzie in 1859 and their second son, John H., who was born in 1861. As the only surviving son and the baby of the family, he was the apple of John and Reliance's eyes.

Prior to the Civil War, Captain Payne sailed on numerous vessels. In 1852, he was master of the new ship *Mountain Wave*, which he took from Boston to San Francisco, arriving there on May 28, 1853. His wife made the trip as well. *Mountain Wave* was 634 tons, owned by Alpheus Hardy and Joshua Sears. That same year, Captain Payne was master of the bark *Jeddo*. In 1854, he was sailing from New York either to Charleston or Mobile. In 1854, he was captain of the new ship *Cowper*, an Alpheus Hardy & Co. vessel. In 1858, Captain Payne was master of the ill-fated *Lamplighter*.[1]

Robert K. Cheney's 1964 book, *Maritime History for the Merrimac*, notes that on August 17, 1863, Captain Payne launched his sixth and latest bark, the *Madelia*, owned entirely by Chatham men and to be commanded by him. When the new ship was ready for her first voyage in 1863, John and Reliance decided to take with them their sixteen-year-old daughter, Madelia, for whom the vessel was named, and young John, then a toddler of

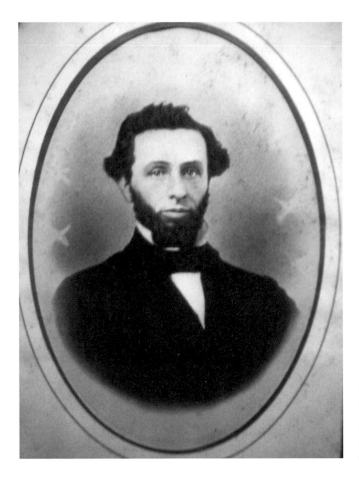

Captain John Payne was master of the bark *Madelia*, named for his eldest daughter. The family, except for two daughters, was lost at sea on her maiden voyage. *Joseph A. Nickerson Jr. Collection.*

two years. Daughters Emma, age six, and Lizzie, age four, were left at home in the care of Judson and Emily Doane, who was Reliance's sister.

Also with Captain Payne and his family on this maiden voyage was young George Nickerson, who was John's nephew and Captain Ziba Nickerson's oldest son. At age eighteen, George was second mate. He would be company for Madelia, too, and that could bring about a close relationship for the future if matters seemed promising between them. All went well on the voyage around the Horn and up to Singapore.

Following is a letter that Reliance wrote to her sister Emily Doane from Hong Kong, dated June 12, 1863:

> *My dear Sister*
>
> *It is seven months to day since wee Sailed from Boston and it seems to have been a much longer time than that to me, but with you the time has passed away and you are now having warm weather at home the Same as it is here all the year around, it is healthy here and not extremely hot as yet, wee lay off about two miles from shore have a nice breeze most of the time which makes it very comfortable…Thare is not anything very attracting on shore So I Spend most of my time on board, sewing and reading.*

*Thin clothing is cheap here, checked Summer Silks 40 cts per yd. I bought Me one the other day if I new you would like one I would get one for you, crape shalls mantillas grass linen Ivray ware, and all kind of chinese goods are cheap compared with the prices at home…Thare are Several English stores here thare goods are all imported from England and the prices higher than Boston, this is a beautiful munday morning I can immagin Myrick getting up Soon as the first peep of day and Starting off for the point & you washing. I think thare must be quite a change to your work this Summer I suppose you See my little girls quite often I long to see them I do not worry about them for I know they are well cared for, I am going to send you Johneys and Delias minature. It is not very good for he would not stand still a second at a time…After you look at it you will send it to fathers, I shall not have time to write father this morning*

*I shall write Some of you every mail long as wee lay here wee have nothing to do yet. Freights are very dull for American vessels. write me when you receive for if wee leave the letters will be forwarded to us.*

*Wee are all well so good Morning.*

This is the only existing letter we have from Reliance or her husband, Captain John Payne. The *Madelia* left Hong Kong for the port of Cebu in the Philippines. From a now lost letter,[2] we know the *Madelia* had arrived in the Philippines. Once the vessel left from Manila bound for San Francisco, it was never heard from again. According to the Hong Kong letter, Emma and Lizzie were being cared for now by Captain and Mrs. Myrick Kent.[3]

Captain John Payne's father was George Payne who had been incarcerated in Dartmoor Prison in the War of 1812. Captain John's sister, Sarah, became the wife of Captain Ziba Nickerson Sr., whose son George was lost at sea on the *Madelia*.

The loss of the brand-new vessel was not only a human tragedy affecting several families in Chatham, but it was a financial disaster as well. The owners of the *Madelia* were all from Chatham. Captain John Payne owned a five sixty-fourths share, the largest of all investors. Samuel Eldredge, Joseph Harding and Christopher Taylor III each held a two sixty-fourths share. The seven remaining investors with a one sixty-fourth share each included Myrick N. Kent, Clement Kendrick, Howes Ryder, Joshua Y. Bearse, Elijah W. Carpenter, James Bearse and Jonathan Eldredge.

Between the loss of the *Madelia* and also the *Lamplighter*, of which Payne had an interest, the Civil War years were not good ones for the Payne family. When the *Lamplighter* was sunk by the *Alabama*, the Payne family, as well as the ship's Boston and Chatham investors, lost a great deal. However, ten years after the incident when a suit was brought against the *Alabama* for the loss of the *Lamplighter* and her cargo, restitution was made. By that time some protagonists were no longer alive, including Captain John Payne.

The New Bedford Library in Massachusetts contains the list of owners with their claims in the suit against the *Alabama*. It notes the following: Loss of the vessel was $13,875 with her freight valued at $3,780 for a total claim of $17,655. Captain John Payne's suit for his loss of stores and personal effects totaled $1,845. On the basis

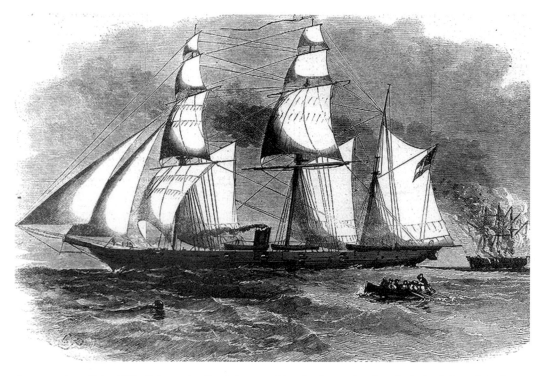

An engraving of the CSS *Alabama*, the Confederate raider that burned and sunk the bark *Lamplighter* in October 1862. Captain Elijah Crosby was her master at one time and Captain Payne owned shares in her. *From* Harper's Weekly, *1862.*

of shares, which each owner held, those with two sixty-fourths were due $578.12, those with one sixty-fourth would be reimbursed $289.06. There is a notation that the skipper, Orrin V. Harding, sued for the loss of personal effects, but no amount is recorded.

Despite most of the family's being lost at sea, they were not forgotten. In the center area of People's Cemetery in Chatham, there is a tall monument bearing a carving of the bark *Madelia*. This monument and the surrounding tombstones tell much about the interconnection of the families affected by the ship's loss.

# JOSIAH HARDY III
## (1822–1902)
### *Captain Turned Lighthouse Keeper*

The role of lighthouse keepers has been romanticized over the years. Josiah Hardy III, born in Chatham in 1822, is probably the most famous of all Chatham lighthouse keepers for two reasons—his twenty-eight years of service and his detailed accounts of the wrecks, the weather and the erosion of James Head, the site of the Twin Lights of Chatham.

However, before his days as lighthouse keeper, he was a skilled sea captain. As was fairly typical in those times, young Josiah began his seafaring life as a cook at the early age of nine years. In reading of these sea captain's lives, one can't help but notice how often children were entrusted with the cooking. Josiah was a young, ambitious fellow and soon became a mate on long Atlantic Ocean voyages. At about age twenty-one, he became master of square-rigged vessels, one of which was the 174-ton brig *Chatham*.

"Captain Josiah Hardy breaks all records. Comes from Africa in 20 days and made the round trip in a little more than two months," reads an 1855 newspaper clipping pasted on the back of an oil painting of the *Brig* Chatham *at Smyrna, Captain Josiah Hardy, 1853*, owned by Mrs. James Hardy.

In 1965, two of Captain Josiah's grandchildren, Grace and Edna Hardy, daughters of his eldest son, James H. Hardy, were still alive. They contributed greatly to our original research and this biographical profile. Grace Hardy recounted how Captain Josiah took his wife Harriet and their small baby Ursula, who was born in 1856, on a voyage of some duration, probably aboard the *Chatham*. When Ursula would normally learn to walk, she was unable to get any footing because the vessel rolled so much. Upon the family's return to dry land, however, when Ursula did learn to walk, family tradition has it that she *ran* everywhere!

Over the twenty-eight years that Captain Josiah was master, he sailed on several of his cousin Alpheus Hardy's ships,[1] including at least three of the firm's famed clipper ships—the *Mountain Wave*, the *Radiant* and the *Ocean Pearl*.

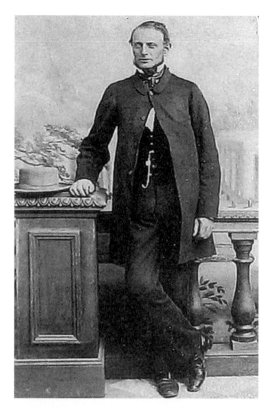

Captain Josiah Hardy when he commanded the ship *Mountain Wave*, which was owned by his cousin Alpheus Hardy. He sailed her to China, Australia and the Philippines. *Courtesy of Mrs. James Hardy.*

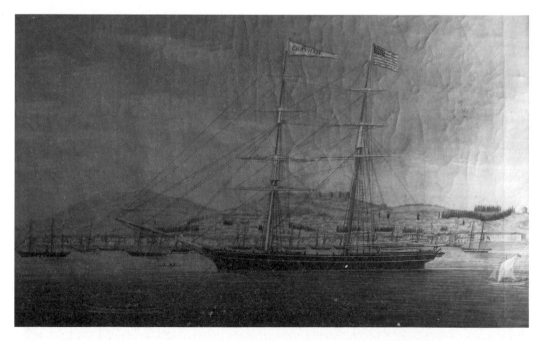

This painting of the 174-ton, square-rigged brig *Chatham*, which was commanded by Captain Hardy when he was just twenty-one years old, clearly shows the harbor of Smyrna, Greece, circa 1853. *Courtesy of Mrs. James Hardy.*

The Hardy sisters related a story about Captain Josiah's stay in Shanghai while his vessel, the *Mountain Wave*, was being repaired. During an insurrection, the captain took aboard two Mandarin Chinese who were being sought by their enemies, and secreted them away until hostilities ceased. The 634-ton ship had excellent stateroom accommodations, so their stay was probably most pleasant. In appreciation for his kindness in providing protection, Captain Hardy was given two carved teak picture frames of great value. Robert Hardy, a great-grandson now living in Chatham, cherishes them. The frames illustrate the story of a young couple who meet (at the bottom of the frame), each goes up a side of the frame, visiting shrines along the way, and they meet at the top center for their marriage ceremony.

At one time Captain Hardy had charge of the ship *Auduban* in which he made a voyage to the Hawaiian Islands. At another time when commanding the *Mountain Wave*, Captain Hardy visited China, Australia, British Columbia and the Philippine Islands. On this trip, which was of nearly five years' duration, he was responsible for the first cargoes of sugar ever taken from the Philippine Island of Panay after its port was opened to commerce in about 1861. He brought that cargo of sugar to New York, arriving in 1862.

Captain Hardy was a man of many enterprises and these were not pursued one at a time, but simultaneously, as records show. The Chatham Town Records[2] document a sale on January l, 1865, where Josiah Hardy paid thirty-five hundred dollars to James H. Tripp and Collins Howes Jr. for the following:

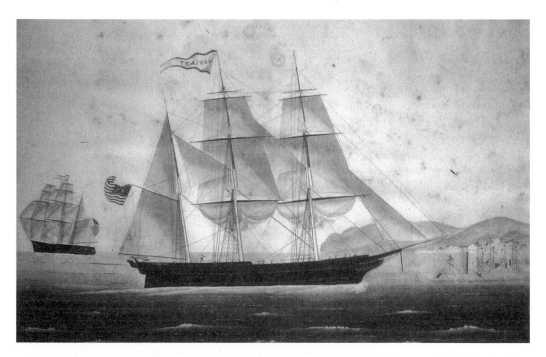

Captain Hardy commanded the bark *Radiant*, shown in this painting entering the Port of Palermo, Italy. Cargoes returning to Boston from this area often included fruit and olive oil. *Joseph A. Nickerson Collection.*

1/16 of Harding's Beach
4/32 of schooner *Charles Reuben*
8/32 of schooner *Water Sprite*
10/32 of schooner *Columbiana*
2/32 of schooner *C. Taylor III*
1/32 of schooner *M.A. Taylor*
4/32 of schooner *Eldorado*
6/32 of schooner *United States*
4/32 of schooner *Emulator*
3/32 of ship *Mary Francis*
4/32 of schooner *Wilde Rose*
and all stores, supplies et cetera.

This store was on a wharf located at the end of Water Street. It carried a variety of articles from clothing, boots, foodstuffs of meal, flour, sugar, lard, salt cod, canned goods and the like, which were available to equip vessels that put in to Chatham on their way either coastwise or for foreign ports. The *Barnstable Patriot* in December 1869 notes:

> *Captain Josiah Hardy has just been filling his pork barrels from the body of a mammoth descendent of those unfortunates who once "ran violently down a steep place into the sea." The weight was about 660 pounds after dressing.*

Captain Josiah Hardy's last command was the 770-ton clipper ship *Ocean Pearl* in which he made a voyage to Farragonia, Spain, at some time in 1871. The *Ocean Pearl* was launched in August 1853 not only to sail fast but to stow a large cargo. It is not clear just what transpired, but due to the neglect of the Spanish customs officials, his ship was wrecked—a total loss. It was a terrible blow to a proud veteran seafarer. Upon his return to Chatham, he retired from sailing altogether and lived to become a legend in his time as the quintessential keeper of the Chatham Lights from 1872 to 1900.

However, by January 11, 1872, the *Chatham Monitor* noted in two separate reports:

> *Captain Josiah Hardy arrived home last week. He has had command of the schooner* Josiah Hardy, *temporarily relieving Capt. Everett Patterson who came home sick. Capt. Patterson has been restored to health and left Monday to assume command of his vessel.*
> *The old store owned by Capt. Josiah Hardy has been partially taken down. The tide has undermined the studding to such an extent as to necessitate its removal.*

One week to the day after that stand-in trip as master was reported, the *Chatham Monitor* of January 18, 1872, announced the beginnings of Captain Hardy's second, noteworthy calling. The report noted his appointment as assistant lighthouse keeper, in place of Ezra Hutchins who resigned. By December 6, 1872, Josiah Hardy was *the* keeper of the Chatham Lights. An interesting recounting of the lighthouse's history was provided at the 1924 summer meeting of the Chatham Historical Society. It was delivered by Grace Hardy.[3] Here are some excerpts:

> *Our first set of lights was built on the bluff called James's Head about where the ruins of the second towers now are. These were finished in 1808...In 1840, a second set of towers was built, this time of brick. Collins Howes was the first keeper, followed by Simeon Nickerson* [who died in 1848]. *After his death his widow* [Angelina Nickerson] *continued as keeper* [for about 12 years or better] *until Charles Smith took them about 1861. On December 6, 1872, Josiah Hardy became keeper after having served one year as assistant keeper. It is from his diary that I have gathered these facts concerning the lighthouses of Chatham.*
>
> *Although the diary recounts an astonishing number of wrecks nearby, with many lives lost, apparently all went well with the lights until 1870. At that time, the mainland extended far beyond the site of the lighthouses and the coast was very bold to the eastward—in some places 40 or 50 feet high. Below this bank were two wharves where the vessels and packets used to load and unload their cargoes.*
>
> *On the 15th of November 1870, a terrific storm came on with north-easterly gales and extremely high tides. All day long the wind and rain increased and the tides ran higher. Faces began to grow anxious, the fisherman made their boats as secure as possible, and all eyes scanned the sea for wrecks and coming danger to the seafarers. Suddenly came the cry, "the beach has broken through!" and sure enough, the angry waves were washing in around the piles of Hardy's wharf. At that time the brick towers stood 228 feet from the edge of the bank.*

By March 31, 1877, the sea had encroached to the point that the distance from the south tower to the sea was only eighty-four feet by actual measurement. The land was falling away fast and by April 25, Frederick Tower, assistant engineer of the lighthouse board, arrived to arrange and lay out the grounds for building a new set of lighthouses on the west side of the road. Miss Grace added that during this time her grandmother, from her kitchen window, and grandfather from the towers, could look almost directly down into the sea, only seventy-seven feet now from the foot of South Tower. The new towers, built of iron outside and brick inside, were set a hundred feet apart and were forty feet high. They were rushed, and on September 6, 1877, the engineers moved the lenses from the old towers to the new ones. The towers were lit on that same night and burned lard oil. It was not until the lanterns were equipped with fixtures for kerosene on July 4, 1878, that the lights burned any other fuel besides lard oil.

The lighthouse keeper's residence for the new towers was completed by November 1877 and Captain Josiah and his family moved in. The old towers, one by one, succumbed to the ravages of the sea, and by 1881 both the old South and North Towers had fallen down the embankment. The old wharves were lost and houses that were down below had either disappeared or been moved up to the new embankment beside the new twin towers.

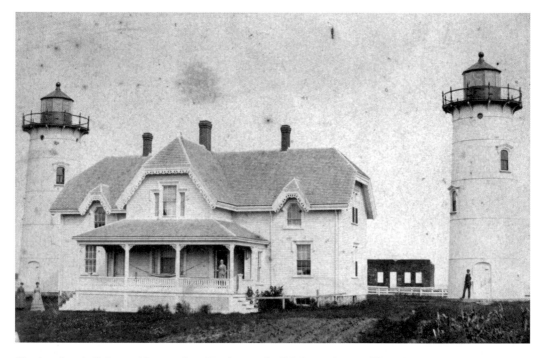

Chatham's twin lights and house when Hardy was the lighthouse keeper. The ruins of the old keeper's house are seen between the house and the lighthouse, *at right*, where Captain Hardy stands. *Courtesy of the Chatham (MA) Historical Society Inc.*

Captain Josiah Hardy remained as "Keeper of the Lights" for twenty-eight years, finally retiring because of ill health. He remained a highly respected citizen of Chatham until his death on November 13, 1902. He and Harriet are buried at Chatham's Seaside Cemetery.

# BENAJAH CROWELL JR.
## (1824–1900)
### *Voyages Chronicled by Wife*

The bark *Wild Rover* is one of the most famous vessels of the nineteenth century. It was owned by the firm of Alpheus Hardy & Co., of Boston, and Captain Benajah Crowell Jr. was her master from 1856 to 1858. It is within that time frame that the greater part of this narrative occurs. Captain Benajah was a man of depth, intellectual curiosity and sensitivity—traits unusual in sea captains of his time. From his sea journal, which is lost except for a few jottings, there is this rather sentimental bit of poetry:

> *Closer, closer, let us knit*
> *Hearts and hands together,*
> *Where our fireside comforts sit,*
> *In the wildest weather*
> *O! They wander wide who roam*
> *For the joys of life from home.*

Also in Benajah Crowell's journal was a list of books to be purchased in Boston: Rollins's *Ancient History*, Locke's *Human Understanding*, Abercrombie's *Intellectual Powers*, Good's *Book of Nature* and Chambers's *Encyclopedia*. That Captain Benajah was also a man who appreciated art is indicated by his observations in the journal when he was laying over in Copenhagen:

> *May 7, 1853: Came to anchor with head wind. Went on Shore to see the town. Called in to the King's Academy of Painting and Statuary. Don't think it equal to the art union at New York; however it has some Splendid paintings. The entrance landing [painting] of Dagmar, first Queen of Denmark by Wegener, I think it a splendid painting. We visited the Museum of Thorwaldsen the great Sculptor, his name is held in great reverence here. The city is scrupulously clean.*

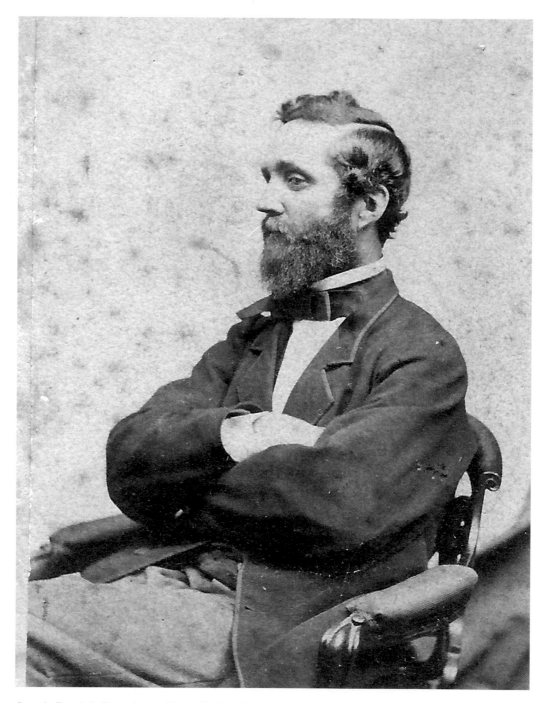

Captain Benajah Crowell posed in profile for this photograph presenting the left side of his face. A hunting accident had damaged his right eye and right arm. *Joseph A. Nickerson Jr. Collection.*

And later the same day:

> *Saw most all of the great men of Europe* [in wax]. *They say they look natural as life almost; I think if they had Washington's figure it would beat them all. They think a great deal of Christian IV but he looks ugly. Napoleon looks noble but Washington would look more like the Great and good than all of them.*

Captain Benajah Crowell's wife, Almira, accompanied him on almost all of his voyages and kept a detailed, newsy diary. Jack Hurlburt, a great-grandson of Almira, his sister Ella Beardsley and their families generously supplied us with the writings, family correspondence and documents from which this account is drawn.

In an 1858 voyage of the bark *Wild Rover*, the captain and Almira took with them their firstborn son, Kleber, who was just three years old. Kleber was so named when he was born at sea on Captain Crowell's earlier vessel, the bark *Kleber*. Almira Crowell's diary documents the days' happenings on this voyage and on subsequent ones as well. Almira's diary is endearing in its detail, reveals much about her, Captain Benajah and son Kleber and offers a glimpse of what it was like to be a family at sea in the nineteenth century.

The *Wild Rover* and company had left Liverpool on February 19, bound for Callao, Peru, with a fair wind. Almira's first entries begin:

> *March 4th: Very pleasant, passed Teneriffe.*

> *March 5th: Blowing a gale from southwest, carried away main and mizzen top gallant sails, sea runs high and bury the ship, water washes into the galley, put the fire out, and made cook cross, washed cook in*[to] *the lee scuppers.*

> *March 7th: At daylight that everlasting Teneriffe under the lee bow, kept off and went south of it, passed the city Santa Cruz at noon, Capt. thought he smelt orange blossoms.*

> *March 8th: Spoke* [flag raised in greeting another vessel] *the Scotch Bark* Pacific *bound to Montevideo, the peak of Teneriffe seen distance of 78 miles, its height 12,172 feet.*

> *March 24th: . . . saw an American ship, passed her during the night, Capt. thought he could beat her, but she passed us, through the day—but she was a full clipper.*

> *March 26th: Very warm, we have met the sun, crossed the line* [Equator] *at 2 P.M.*

> *April 1st: Nearly calm, saw the Ship* Detroit *of Yarmouth, N.S.*

> *April 2nd: . . . The whale ship* Lydia *of New Bedford hove in sight, Capt. Leonard came on board, gave him all our Boston papers, he had been forty months from home, we were all so taken up with him that we didn't think of writing home.*

By April 24 there was a shortage of water on board and Almira wrote, "…allowance of water; gallon a man, 3 qts. for cooking, l for washing and drinking."

*May 7th: It has been very rough and been obliged to keep in my berth, it was too much for Kleber…he tried to play—if he cant keep his balance and finds he is going to the leeward, he will sit down and slide across the room.*

*May 11th: Unless it rains we will have to put in short of Callao (for water), two sails in company with us, one is a Callao packet from Havre, two men sick, one fell and hurt him, the other has a fever.*

*May 14th: Kleber's 4th birthday; the Tinker made him a trumpet [and] he was on deck all day singing out "splice the main brace" and "about ship."*

*May 15th: Sea was rising and wind braying. I could parch no more [popcorn] as it grew so rough, they would roll off the stove and down behind the coal box. Gus made some molasses corn, then attempted to make some candy, he boiled it all the afternoon, and as it was done the bottom of the tin came out (that the tinker made the day before) and all went into the fire; Capt. came down thinking he'd get some candy but got disappointed; wind increasing, at 6 P.M. under close reefed topsails, and hove to at 8, blew a gale all night.*

Augustus, Almira's fourteen-year-old brother whom everyone called Gus, had received the popcorn from his mother. Gus was brought on the trip as cabin boy—a common practice for many seagoing families. For many youngsters, it was their introduction to life at sea.

*May 23rd: Expect to see land after dinner, it seems like getting home, to make preparations for port, Gus put down the carpet.*

*May 26th: Capt. of the port (San Lorenzo) came on board, Benajah went on shore, found Capt. Kelly of the* Osborne Howes, *Sears of* Conquest, *Gardner of* John Bryant *and Reynolds of* Georgianna, *plenty of other ships and nothing to do.*

*May 29th: The* Osborne Howes *sails for Boston, Benajah went on board to see him off, brought Capt. Sears and Crowell of the* Ocean Pearl *to dinner.*

*June 1st: Jimmy Burr came on and spent the day with Kleber, Mrs. Taylor came and spent the evening; Capt. Sears and Reynolds came also.*

*June 4th: Benajah, Kleber, Capt. and Mrs. Taylor and myself started for Lima went on shore to Callao…then rode in the English cars through sand and fields the distance of 10 miles and arrived at Lima, went through a Catholic church; went down to a hotel saw a grand procession of negroes and white men, celebrating the birth of Christ, got dinner came home at 6.*

Almira described much socializing among the captains and their ladies: teas, horseback riding in the hills, dinners in one vessel or another, on one occasion going to a bullfight, shopping and the like. Following is her description of their Fourth of July:

*All the harbor Americans met on board the* Star King, *Capt, Crabtree's vessel to celebrate the 4th—we had a grand dinner, speeches, toasts, a band of music dancing and singing, salutes fired at sunset.*

The vessels stayed in port longer than we may have realized. The *Wild Rover*, on this trip, had come into port on May 24 and did not leave until November 5, when she left Callao for Hampton Roads. By Thanksgiving Day, the bark was under double reefs,

*cooking turkey for cabin, killed a pig and making sea pie for forecastle, Ben says he always takes dinner with his family on Thanksgiving Day, after carving the turkey he takes his plate and eats with me and Kleber. We thought the folks at home at their dinner wouldn't think we were enjoying ourselves so well.*

*Nov. 26th: Still blowing and we are fast nearing Cape Horn; I have taken a severe cold in my face, the wind blowing in through the cracks—use gin and flour to draw it out.*

*Nov. 27th: Ship rolling heavy, everything that is loose is flying in every direction. Kleber is trying to amuse himself about the cabin, sometimes he is sliding across the floor as the ship rolls, says he thinks the wharf will come soon; he is not aware what a long track we are to sail before we reach home, he dreams every night of the wharf and seeing Emma* [Kleber's Hardy grandmother, Almira's mother].

*Dec 14th: Capt. 34th birthday, he is going to leave off tobacco; Kleber has a habit of biting his nails, says he is going to leave that off too.*

*Dec. 16th: Cap, using tobacco as ever, Kleber biting his nails. I ask him if he has forgotten his promise, says papa hasn't left off tobacco.*

By January 4, 1859, they were well on their way home.

*Yesterday Benajah's game cock was sitting on the rail taking a view of the water when the wind from the mainsail blew him overboard, and was drowned, too bad Kleber says, can't carry him to Granpa Hardy.*

*Jan. 5th:…about 20 miles from Pernambuco [Brazil], see the land and buildings very plain; very hot—Kleber takes a nap on the cabin floor; Charley—one of the men, made him a pair of canvas slippers which he wears without any stockings, he has worn his shoes nearly all up, keeping one pair to wear home.*

*Benajah says we are having a long passage and I am afraid we shall be obliged to put in for provisions. I tell him I wouldn't as long as we have beef and bread, for I can live on that as long as anybody; Tonight steward says we are getting short of tea, sir, well says the captain, don't let the tea get out unless you want to get out yourself, give the men coffee, as we have plenty.*

*Crossed the line* [Equator] *last night at 10 had a heavy shower of rain, Benajah got wet through, Kleber sings sailor songs while pulling off papa's boots.*

*Jan. 12th: Went out to breakfast and behold we had flying fish for breakfast, quite a treat fresh fish; Kleber goes on the main deck through the dog watch, to play the band as he calls it, he with an old tin pot and carpenter with symbols.*

*Jan. 26th: 80 miles from Cape Henry, all hands wishing a fair wind, especially the tobacco chewers.*

*Jan. 27th: Burnt blue lights and rockets, part (of) the night for a pilot, but none until morning, anchored at Hampton Roads at noon, Ben gone to Norfolk for orders.*

*Jan.30th: Kleber and I sailed in the steamer* Joseph Whitney *for Boston; from Baltimore passed father's* [Chatham] *in the morning of the 4th of February, arrived in Boston at night, spent two days in Boston and landed home safe, after fifteen month's absence.*

In a letter to her parents, Almira told them that, although Benajah urged her to stay home with the children, she knew that it was he who needed her most. Almira Hardy Crowell wanted to be with her husband and she was sure that he was considerably healthier and happier when she was with him. It is also evident that Almira loved being at sea—which was so much more exciting than being at home—and she liked the added pleasure of being waited on and having all the cooking and housekeeping done for her.

She mentioned a voyage to Batavia—now Jakarta, Indonesia—in a letter to her mother on December 16, 1861. It could have been written only by a woman of Almira's mettle. Their son Herbert, who had been born just two years earlier, was with them. Almira wrote, in part:

*Last Sunday, the 9th, Benajah, Herbert and I went out to ride, we came back at 8 o'clock and at 10 I had a little girl, we are both very well, or much better than I expected in this hot climate, though it is no hotter than our climate in July or August.*

The baby girl was just one day old when she was presented with a tiny piece of paper from the steward. Almira recorded this touching and gallant present in her diary:

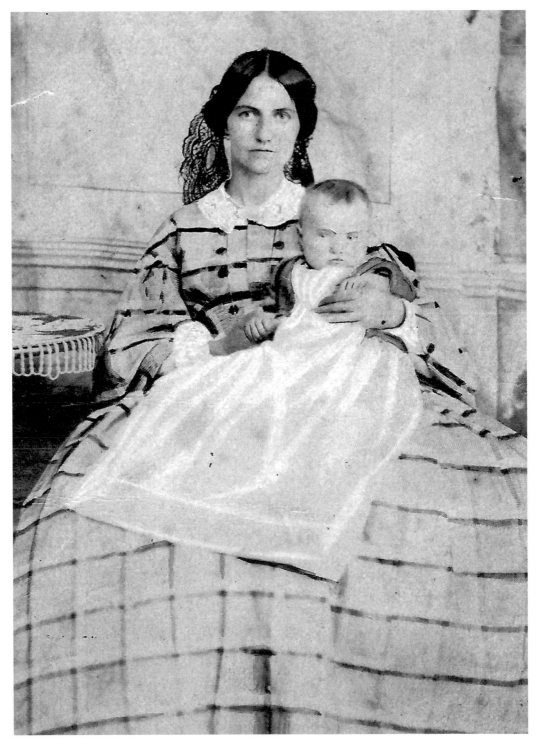

Almira Crowell with her six-month-old daughter Ella, who was born December 9, 1861, during the *Wild Rover*'s stopover in Batavia, Java. *Joseph A. Nickerson Jr. Collection.*

*Wild Rover, Dec.14, 1861 To Miss Crowell, With the compliments of the Steward who hopes the young lady will not take offense at the nature of the gift from one who wishes her all prosperity and over all things trusts she may never live to need a gift of either socks or shoes. Respectfully, W. Bradford*

Later Almira wrote:

*Don't dare undertake much, because it is not so easy getting well as it is to keep well. I am glad to get through and not detain the ship. Benajah said he would not go until I was well if the ship was ready, but I shall be ready before the ship, the Dr. says it will be perfectly safe for me to go on board the 23rd and the ship will not be ready until about the 25th…the boat will come up the canal below the hotel and go direct to the ship so it will be no trouble going on board.*

Almira added that she had an English doctor, the landlady and two native women assist in the birth. There was a picture of the very proper document attesting to the birth of her daughter, Ella, and Almira assured her mother that if there was no female servant appropriate for hire they would find a "China boy," because she wanted somebody on board the ship to wash diapers and such things! She said that the steward had volunteered to nurse, and that he would be a good one if he didn't have any other duties to attend to, but she assured her mother that she had plenty of help.

On one occasion, the captain told Almira that the owners had seemed less than happy that he had his wife and son aboard, at which she wrote to her mother,

*If the owners find fault with this, I shall tell them next time the Capt. will take his wife, his wife's sister and four children, though relatives are never allowed so much as other people.*

She ended by sending love to all the "family of Hardys, both sides of the street…"

Several months later, Almira wrote from the port of Batavia on March 23, 1862, en route to Bremen, which had taken an unexpected ninety days to reach.

*We spoke and boarded the bark* Hebron, *Capt. Witham from Cadix for Montevideo March 8th in the Doldrums, the Capt. came on board brought us papers, the latest from June 11th which have been read and reread all over the ship, also a Dutch flag in case we are chased by the* Sumpter.

That is the only reference Almira makes to the Civil War in her letters.

There are no other vessels associated with Captain Benajah Crowell Jr., except the earlier *Kleber.* The bark *Wild Rover* seemed to be his favorite vessel. Our records do not tell at what time the captain and his lady decided that they would forsake the sea for Chatham's *terra firma*. By the time of the following article in the *Chatham Monitor* of January 17, 1882, Captain and Mrs. Crowell were back in Chatham.

*Capt. Benajah Crowell is circulating a petition for the removal of the weather signal station to some more favorable position near the shore to be more readily seen from the sea, and in case that is done, asks that he may be the keeper. Capt. Crowell is well acquainted from personal experience with all that belongs to the life of a sailor and is no doubt fully competent to perform the duties of this office.*

When Benajah purchased their Chatham home, now 352 Main Street, it was one of the finest estates in Chatham. Built by Isaac Hardy, Almira's grandfather, the house, recently restored, is directly across from the Cranberry Inn. The captain and Almira had six children. The captain died in 1900; Almira in 1909. The family is buried in Union Cemetery.

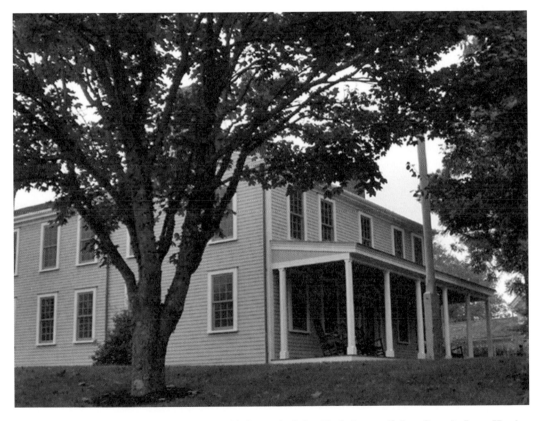

Benajah and family lived on Main Street in this house, built by Almira's grandfather, Captain Isaac Hardy. The house has recently been transformed from an inn to a private home again. *Photograph by Janet M. Daly.*

# DAVID SMITH
## (1824–1886)
### Sea Captain Turned Ice Mogul

S ome of you who read this account of Captain David Smith may remember the days when your family had an icebox at home. You would put a card in the window to say how much ice was needed that day—twenty-five pounds, fifty pounds or more—and ice was delivered right to your door. That was possible because of the good Captain Smith! Until Frigidaires and Kelvinators entered our kitchens, we were all in need of the wonderful ice-making machine for which David Smith owned the patents.

As one article in 1883 said, the patents made possible "the novel process whereby the product of sturdy Old Winter is made to appear in midsummer." The *Washington Evening Star* carried an article that told, in detail, the process of ice making and "what Captain David Smith is doing towards getting the luxuries of the polar regions down towards the tropics." The *Evening* Star added, "There will be no excuse now for Congressmen not keeping their cool."

But how and why David Smith became interested in ice making will come later. Let's begin at the beginning. David's father, Stephen Smith, was a prosperous farmer who wanted his eldest son to be a lawyer. David, on the other hand, wanted the adventure of going to sea. His father arranged with a "friendly shipmaster" to take David on a voyage to "give him a taste of wholesome ship discipline" in the hope that he would be cured of wanting to go to sea. David returned from his maiden voyage more determined than ever to make the sea his life. In 1844 and 1845, David served as a mate, gaining experience plying the coastal seas on the schooner *J. & L. Erickson* between Boston and Philadelphia, and Philadelphia and Charleston.

David married Patience "Patia" Ryder in 1847 and started making plans toward building a ship of his own. In 1850, Patia Ryder died two days after giving birth to their daughter, Patia. While David was ashore awaiting the birth of their first child, he worked as a carpenter. His account book records work on the meetinghouse, houses, barns and bridges. He was single-minded in raising the funds to build his ship.

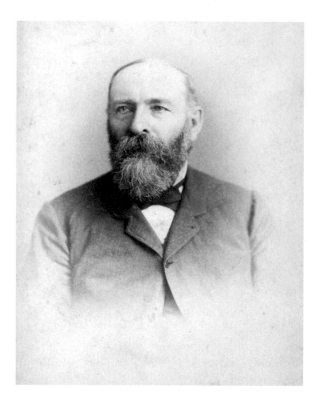

Captain David Smith, circa 1867, dreamed of his own vessel. He built the *Maria J. Smith*, a bark named for his second wife. Her death prompted his ice-making business. *Courtesy of David Foster, a direct descendant of Captain Smith.*

To this end, David also owned a business with Samuel Armstrong on Old Wharf Road in North Chatham. It canned and hermetically sealed provisions such as clams, lobster, fish, et cetera, and sold to both wholesale and retail customers. This enterprise ended when the firm, Smith & Armstrong, was sold to Asa Nye in 1857. At the same time, David sold the building that housed the company to his father for fifteen hundred dollars and, for good measure, also included "3,000 cans of sealed goods."

Stephen Smith was reputed to be the richest man in Chatham. In those days, there were few banks and everybody invested their money in land or shipping—or else kept it under their beds. Father Stephen was known at times to have as much as fifty thousand dollars in gold stored in a trunk beneath his four-poster. (Today that sum would be the equivalent of about one and a half million dollars!)

While his bark was still in the dreaming stages, David made a whaling voyage to the Pacific and Arctic Oceans. It was clear, however, that whaling didn't have the same attraction for young David as did later voyages of commerce that took him around the world.

Leroy and Evelyn Foster of Chatham (Mrs. Foster was a direct descendent of David Smith) shared David's log with us. The log begins with a voyage to Havana and that portion is more concerned with the winds, the course, the rigging of the sails, et cetera, for each twenty-four-hour block. He wrote of "jentle breezes," "severall sail in sight" and "the vesul having been sold to the Spanish authorities, the American flag was halled down…The crew were sent on shor to the American counsuls…" Then, David said, the vessel's captain and officers came back to the States via the packet SS *United States.*

Later on in the log, David says *Splendid* was the whaling vessel on which he sailed to the Bering Straits, the Arctic Ocean, the southwestern seas and New Zealand. The ship embarked from Cold Spring Harbor on Long Island, New York.[1]

By 1854, David had married a second wife, Maria Armstrong of Deer Island, New Brunswick. When daughter, Anna Maria, was born in 1856, David was listed as a carpenter; in 1857, at daughter Emma's birth, David was listed in *Chatham's Vital Records* as a schoolteacher. In 1858, when their third daughter, Harriet, was born, David was back at sea. By 1859, he had become Captain David Smith, skipper of the schooner *Mary E. Smith,* carrying commercial freight between Philadelphia and Mobile.

By 1862, the vessel of his dreams was about to become a reality. A contract memorandum, dated May 1, 1862, between Toby and Littlefield, shipbuilders of Portsmouth, New Hampshire, and David Smith of Chatham, Massachusetts, master mariner, was for twenty-one thousand dollars. David's log contains a highly detailed description of the bark *Maria J. Smith,* which was named for his wife. Included were instructions for the forward cabin to be painted, the after cabin finished in hard wood and upon the main deck "to be built a house for the accommodation of crew and galley." The memo called for five thousand dollars in cash to be paid when lower deck beams were in, and the balance when she was launched and delivered. Toby and Littlefield agreed to take one-quarter share of the bark they built for David Smith "to be sailed by him on shares at equal halves without primage." By the time the *Maria J. Smith* was equipped and ready, thirty-four thousand dollars had been invested by the following individuals:

| Owner | # Shares | $ Amount |
|---|---|---|
| David Smith | 19 | $10,093.00 |
| Toby & Littlefield | 16 | $8,500.00 |
| Stephen Smith (Father) | 8 | $4,250.00 |
| Messrs. Godfrey & Holyoke | 3 | $1,593.75 |
| Howes Ryder | 4 | $2,125.00 |
| Maurice M. Pigott | 1 | $531.25 |
| Henry G. Reeves | 5 | $2,656.25 |
| Mark Googins | 2 | $1,062.50 |
| Messrs. Bagnal & Loud | 1 | $531.25 |
| Messrs. Crocker & Otis | 3 | $1,593.75 |
| Messrs. Pigeon & Odiorne | 2 | $1,062.50 |
| | 64 | $33,999.25 |

To identify some of the owners: Howes Ryder was a friend of David's father; Pigeon & Odiorne furnished extra sails, spare topmast and lower yard; Crocker & Otis were the sailmakers; Mark Googins was the blacksmith; and Mr. Loud provided the blocks on which the vessel rested until her launching.

On her maiden voyage to Montevideo in the late fall of 1862 she carried an assorted cargo, passengers from New York, David's wife Maria and their three little girls. For seven years, Captain Smith made long voyages to ports all over the world with excellent returns. In just two years during the Civil War, Captain Smith alone earned seventy thousand dollars as his share from the *Maria J. Smith.*

In 1864, the captain's wife Maria was with him on a voyage to Bassene, Burma, where she fell ill and died of cholera. David was devastated. The attending physician told him that if there had been sufficient ice on hand Maria might have recovered. This untimely death of his wife, more than anything else, spurred him on to explore a means of manufacturing ice, especially for its use in tropical climates such as Bassene. While naturally frozen ice had been exported in the nineteenth century from the States even as far as Peking, China, it was not available in any great quantity in many areas of the world, including the United States.

The *Maria J. Smith* made a voyage from New York to Europe via Australia, China and the East Indies in 1865. Captain Smith returned to the West Coast in 1868, with a cargo bound for Seattle. His vessel was being towed by tug into the harbor when a violent storm developed. The tug cut the vessel loose and the *Maria J. Smith* went onto the rocks. Worse, her insurance had been allowed to lapse. David was so upset by the loss—not only for himself, but for his family and friends who owned stock in his vessel—that he refused to return home until he was able to repay the losses. It took him nine years.

The *Maria J. Smith* was repaired and Captain David accepted a charter from San Francisco to the Chincha Islands, off the Peruvian coast. His account book noted, on September 4, 1869, that the vessel was in debt, but that voyage put him on the road to solvency. A round-trip voyage to Australia paved the way for his leaving the sea.

While in California, he had bought patents of an existing ice-making machine, but worked out his own plans for a machine for which he applied and received patents. Then he spent four years in Honolulu working toward perfecting his ice machine. A clipping from the *Harwich Independent*, reprinted in the *Chatham Monitor*, dated January 21, 1875, notes:

> *Captain David Smith is in San Francisco arranging for new machinery to be used in his business of ice manufacturing at the Sandwich Islands* [today's Hawaiian Island chain]. *His wife* [this would be his third wife, Susan] *is also with him.*

In 1877, the time of his homecoming, his ice company was a success with machines operating in Cuba, Honolulu, Caracas, Oakland, California, and in several Southern states. From the time that he came east, Captain David devoted all of his time and effort to perfecting his ice-making machines and their distribution over a good part of the world. He and his wife Susan E. Smith, with their son George and two daughters Patia and Harriett, took up residence in Washington, D.C. His manufacturing plant there—in what is now Georgetown—was highly successful and given much publicity. This article appeared in the *National Free Press* and was reprinted in the *Cape Cod Item* of June 1883.

*We copy the following…knowing it will interest Capt. Smith's townspeople. "The Smith Transparent Ice Company was established here [Washington, DC] in the Fall of 1881, with only one machine for the manufacture of Transparent ice. The demand has steadily increased until now…they have four machines in full operation and ten wagons on the streets. A distinguished State chemist says: 'I have examined samples of the Ice…and take great pleasure in recommending it to the public…no Ice more wholesome than this is to be had.'*

*"With such an endorsement, we are not surprised at the rapid strides this company has made. They have made no fuss about it, have not heralded it abroad that they manufacture an article superior to nature's gift, but quietly and unostentatiously put the article on the market to stand or fall upon its merits, with the result above stated, which must be exceedingly gratifying to those who conceived and carried into effect the measure which has thus far received the unqualified endorsement of the people.*

*"Under the excellent management of Mr. David Smith, the company has prospered and will no doubt continue to flourish and grow rich under his supervision."*

David brought his family into the firm. His brother Rufus, and Rufus's twin sons, Morris and Curtis, as well as their brother Maurice, were all active in setting up manufacturing locations. Curtis was in Raleigh, North Carolina. A short column in the *Chatham Monitor*, dating from July 12, 1881, notes:

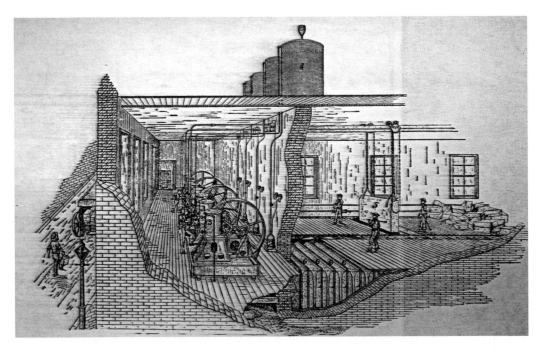

A schematic of the Smith Transparent Ice Factory shows how ice was made in congealing boxes using a process involving ammonia to freeze the water into blocks of ice. *Joseph A. Nickerson Jr. Collection.*

*Mrs. David Smith of this town, now of Washington [DC], was a witness from a window across the street of the attempted assassination of the President [James Garfield]*[2] *and saw the would-be murderer marched away.*

The Smiths considered Chatham their home base, but the men traveled a great deal due to the ice business. An unmarked Cape Cod newspaper clipping in 1884 noted that Maurice, living in Washington, D.C.,

*has been visiting his home at Chathamport a few days. He now goes to New Orleans to remain during the* [1884 World's Industrial and Cotton Centennial] *Exposition in that city in charge of the Smith Transparent Ice Co.'s exhibit.*

Captain David Smith died on December 13, 1886, of heart failure. He was in New Orleans supervising the building of what was to be the largest ice-making machine in the world at that time, capable of manufacturing a hundred tons of ice per day. His obituary, as it appeared in the *Chatham Monitor*, shows the respect with which he was remembered at his death:

*A young man of integrity, honesty and sterling worth, characteristics, which he carried with him all through life. He was a member of the Congregational Church, taught in its Sabbath School, was a member of the church choir and was a deacon of the church. Funeral services were conducted at the home of his brother, Rufus. He was 62 years of age.*

# JOHN TAYLOR III
## (1824–1886)
### *Master of the* Red Cloud

On a high bluff in Brewster overlooking Cape Cod Bay once stood the rather crudely carved figure of a woman. Seen against a sunset, she seemed a figure of spirit and grace—as if wind was blowing her drapery and streaming hair. For twenty-five years, this was the figurehead of the good ship *Imperial*. Built in Quincy in 1869 by "Deacon" George Thomas, the *Imperial* was owned by Isaac Taylor of Boston, originally of Chatham. On her first voyage—Boston to Singapore via London—Captain John Taylor III, Isaac's nephew, was her master.

Young John was another precocious captain-to-be when he went to sea at eleven years old. His grandfather John and his father, John Taylor Jr., had been sea captains, and John III had three other siblings—Horace, Prince and Simeon—who also became captains. As the eldest of the four boys, his eagerness to join the ranks as a full-fledged mariner set an example for his brothers.

There is an account that sheds light on these lads' taking to the high seas at very early ages. It comes from Rear Admiral Charles A. Rockwell's *Autobiography of a Seaman* in which he describes the vessels, their admirable conditions aboard and notes that on each training voyage there were eight to twelve youngsters who stood out. They were marked for prospective mates, then masters of vessels, when they attained the experience, appropriate age and achievement. That is the formula that shaped John's preparation for master, consistent with maritime training in New England at the time.

John married Elizabeth Mayo in 1847. He had chosen a wife who enjoyed sailing with her husband. In fact, Elizabeth accompanied him on more than forty sea voyages, crossing the equator twenty-eight times. The couple had two daughters and six sons. Two of the boys were born at sea—their third son, Edgar Rockland, was born in 1855 aboard the ship *Rockland*, and fifth son, Freddie Imperial, was born in 1870 on board the ship *Imperial*. With their middle names, they weren't ever going to forget their birthplaces!

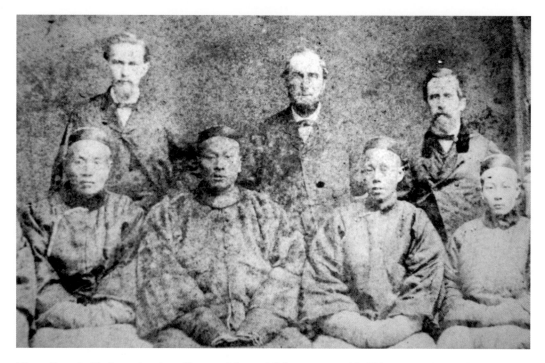

Three Captain Taylors—brothers Simeon, John and Prince—pose with Chinese merchants circa 1860, when all three were ashore at the same time. *Courtesy of Helen Monroe Johnson, Simeon's granddaughter.*

While official records abound telling what vessels our sea captains commanded and to and from what ports they traveled, there are few glimpses into their ships' holds to see what was carried from port to port. However, we found a record of one of Captain John Taylor's cargoes when he commanded the brig *Oak* and left Boston in July 1851 bound for Gibraltar. The brig was carrying:

100 barrels of beef
81 packages of glassware
l bale of chairs
9 more packages of glassware
25 bales of cotton
82 boxes of tobacco
24 bales of general merchandise
6 more packages of glassware
and 2,961 pieces of logwood.

On the return to Boston from Gibraltar his cargo list was:

565 bars of lead
62 bales of wool

18 bales of cork
1 box containing saddles
4,500 boxes of raisins
1,500 halves raisins
and 1,015 quarters raisins.

On another trip from Boston to Gibraltar in 1851, Captain Taylor's ship carried:

50 casks of tobacco
177 boxes of same
55 bales of cotton
20 boxes sample hides
40 tons logwood
and 3 boxes of shoes.

The *Chatham Monitor* on August 25, 1872, wrote:

> *Captain John Taylor, of the Ship* Imperial, *arrived at London on the 8th. His wife who accompanied him will return home about September 1st. It is expected that Captain Taylor will assume command of a large clipper ship of 2200 tons, now building, unless she is sold.*

The clipper ship mentioned wasn't sold. It was the *Red Cloud* that was under construction in the Quincy Yard of "Deacon" George Thomas and was built with the aid of John's uncle, Captain Isaac Taylor. Captain John Taylor became the first skipper of the *Red Cloud* when she was launched on November 1877. The *Yarmouth Register* on March 9, 1878, reported:

> *The Ship* Red Cloud, *which will shortly load with wheat at Boston, for Liverpool, was launched at Quincy Point last November, and it is said to be one of the largest and best ships launched from Boston for many years. Her length overall is 252 feet; her breadth of beam 43 feet, depth of hold 26 feet, tonnage 2,208. She will be commanded by Captain John Taylor of Chatham, who supervised her construction. The* American *and* Triumphant *are sister ships of the* Red Cloud *and were built by the same firm.*

An item of March 3, 1882, in the Chatham column of the *Cape Cod Item* read: "Mrs. John Taylor went to Liverpool to meet her husband, Captain Taylor who is soon expected to arrive in his Ship *Red Cloud.*" And, the *Chatham Monitor* added: "She will also meet her son, Walter F. Taylor, who is in business in Liverpool." While Mrs. Taylor was traveling east from Chatham on the steamer *Nova Scotia*, the *Red Cloud* was going west from San Francisco to Liverpool. En route, the *Red Cloud* picked up eight shipwrecked men from the St. Johns, New Brunswick, bark *Fanny B.*, which had burned at sea.

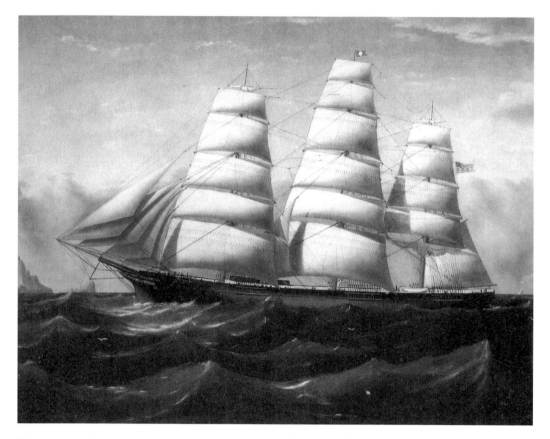

This painting illustrates a three-masted, square-rigged ship very similar to the *Imperial* commanded by John Taylor III and on which his son Freddie Imperial was born. *Joseph A. Nickerson Jr. Collection.*

The *Red Cloud* was a large vessel, requiring a thirty-two-man crew. When she arrived in Liverpool from San Francisco it had been necessary to hire 110 men over the course of the three-year voyage in order to keep the full number of the crew constant. Men jumped ship at various ports of call or were lost overboard or fell to the deck from the rigging. Of these, the greater number jumped ship. Upon arrival in Liverpool, there were only three men of the original crew remaining: Captain Taylor, his first mate and the carpenter. Upon going ashore, the carpenter slipped and fell onto the dock and was killed.

The *Red Cloud* was literally sold out from under the captain while he was in Liverpool. He and Mrs. Taylor came back to Chatham, via New York. Captain John had been absent from home just days shy of four years in command of the *Red Cloud*. She was sold to a German firm and renamed the *Carl Friedrich*. According to the Mariner's Museum in Newport News, Virginia, the ship was

*stranded November 1893 and was condemned, according to Lloyd's Register 1894–95. However she was apparently salvaged and sold because in the supplement to the 1894–95 volume she reappears as* Red Cloud *ex* Carl Friedrich *ex* Red Cloud *built 1878 at Quincy. She is listed as* Red Cloud *in the 1895–96 volume, but disappears without explanation in the 1896–97 volume.*

Before his worldwide travels, Captain Taylor had been engaged in coastal runs between Boston and Philadelphia for several years. One of his early vessels in 1851 was the brig *Chicopee*, followed by the brig *Oak* and the ships *Imperial* and *Star of the West*.

Captain John Taylor might have been an exacting master. In his book, *Sea Yarns*, Captain Joshua Taylor tells about being on a voyage on the bark *Sea Bird* with Captain John in command.

> *I made this trip while in my teens, and the voyage was out to Cape Town from Boston and return. Our crew consisted of six men and four boys before the mast. The chief officer was a brother of the Captain, Prince Harding Taylor by name, and a man by the name of Harding as second mate, all officers hailing from Chatham, Mass. The Captain had his wife and two children with him, one a boy about seven years of age and the other a babe of eighteen months. The Captain was a big, powerful man, very nervous and always finding fault with someone, or something, and his special trouble was the weather. When it was fine, we were going to have a storm, and when it was fair wind it would not last long, and so on, day in and day out, always in a stir. Now the Captain happened to be a cousin of mine, and was always pleasant with me, and would often come and chat with me while I had a trick at the wheel. But should any officer or man suddenly make his appearance he would damn me and order me to mind my course and not be star-gazing around, and I would always answer, "Aye, aye, Sir."*

It was further noted that when "master of the *Sea Bird*, a vessel of 450 tons, Captain Taylor had his crew organized as though they were on a 2,000-ton ship and the routine and discipline were similar."

The *Chatham Monitor* kept everyone abreast of the latest news. This item appeared on April 15, 1875:

> *Letters have been received from Captain John Taylor, of ship* Star of the West *at Manila. He has a valuable cargo—the freight amounting to $65,000—and has sailed for Liverpool. All well.*

Captain John Taylor was a master mariner until three years before he died in 1886. He had circumnavigated the globe a host of times and was a member of the Boston Marine Society. He lived a full and satisfying life surrounded by a large, devoted family. His wife, Elizabeth, lived until 1910.

The family plot is in Chatham's Seaside Cemetery where John, Elizabeth and family are buried.

# SIMEON N. TAYLOR
## (1826–1898)
### *China River Trade*

S imeon N. Taylor was one of John Taylor Jr.'s four sons, who comprise a veritable royal dynasty of Chatham sea captains. He was bright, resourceful, amusing, outspoken, clearheaded, loving and knew his craft to a marked degree in a business full of superlatively qualified peers. His letters to his wife show us why she adored him, and why any woman might wish they had been written to her.

The recipient of his letters was Mehitable "Hitty" Atkins, whom Simeon married in 1848. Hitty was the daughter of Joseph and Fear (Nickerson) Atkins of Chatham. Simeon's only son, Joseph Atkins Taylor, died when he was two years old. The couple had two daughters, Emma and Maria, who were taken on several voyages with their parents.

Captain Taylor's first years at sea were not auspicious. His coasting trips, some of which used to take him past the backside of the Cape, were enlivened by a signal that Hitty flew from their house in Chatham—a sight the captain could sometimes see as he sailed past. He learned the coasting business on the barks *Ella* and *Radiant* before he got his master's ticket. The trips were chiefly to Baltimore, Philadelphia and Charleston.

In 1855, he was in command of the bark *Laconia*, trying in vain to make money by carrying coal and pig iron from Philadelphia to Boston. He wrote:

> *Times are very dull. I do not have anything to do but just set down in Mr. Cooper's counting room* [in Philadelphia] *and drink ice water and smoke cigars. Last evening Atkins and Lewis and myself went down street and went into a Bath House. Elish* [Atkins] *came very near getting into the Ladies' apartment. Think I shall leave off going to sea and buy a farm.*

He often threatened in his letters to quit the sea for a farm. On another occasion he wrote to his wife, "I don't know how the devil it is freights are always dull when I come here [Baltimore], I think I must be a Jonas [*sic*] or something else." By the end of 1855,

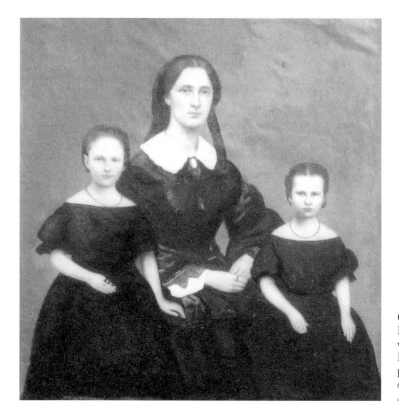

Captain Simeon's wife, Mehitable Taylor, poses with her young daughters Emma and Maria for this portrait, circa 1860. *Courtesy of Helen Monroe Johnson, Simeon's granddaughter.*

however, his luck changed. Howes & Co. offered Captain Simeon the command of the bark *Ella* that was in the Mediterranean fruit trade. He describes a less than romantic life at sea in this letter to Hitty written on the morning of December 21, 1856, as the *Ella* left New York for the Mediterranean. Christmas would be spent away from his family on the high seas.

> *We are now going down with a fair wind, and a bitter cold morning. I will assure you Hitty, I am homesick as a dog…our sails are all frozen and the ropes are all like iron. The mate, he is cross at the sailors.*

In 1857, Captain Simeon was master of the brig *Granada*, also owned by Howes & Co. He took several more voyages to the Mediterranean for the fruit trade, then a trip to Matanzas, Cuba, carrying, of all things, a locomotive under his hatches. He had never been to the island before and was apprehensive about that, but he was even more concerned about unloading the locomotive. He wrote to his wife from Matanzas on February 12, 1858:

> *I am well and hearty and enjoy myself finely…Capt. Nickerson of Dennis, of the Brig J. Nickerson is here. Matanzas is not much of a place anyhow. We have got clear of our Locomotive all right and nobody hurt, thank the Lord…Tell Lucy I am afraid she*

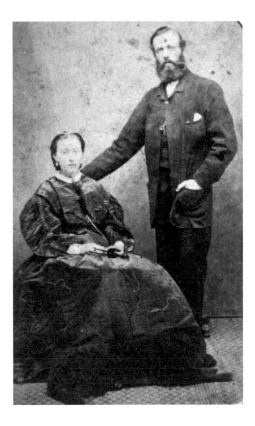

An older Mehitable and Simeon Taylor pose for this photograph with their dog at Hitty's feet, circa 1875. *Courtesy of Helen Monroe Johnson, Simeon's granddaughter.*

*will not get her Bay Rum, for they do not know anything about that kind of rum. I guess they are pretty well posted on the other kind of rum.*

In 1858, still master of the *Granada*, he sailed to Bangkok—his first voyage to Southeast Asia—leaving New York in June with five passengers and a cargo of heavy machinery. "We are nearly unloaded without any damage. I tell you, Hitty, I never want another such cargo to handle. Some pieces weighing 13 tons." Soon after his arrival, Howes & Co. ordered the captain to stay in the East and under no condition to bring the *Granada* home. He was to keep the vessel busy trading locally as long as he could find freights, then sell her and come home.

Following the owner's orders, Captain Simeon found a cargo of rice, sugar and sappan wood[1] in Bangkok to take to Shanghai. As he was about ready to sail, his crew deserted. He took on a native crew, two of whom brought along their wives and children. His own mate, Mr. Ryder, now had to give orders to a bilingual native mate, and the native mate relayed orders to the crew. The arrangement worked so well that the *Granada* reached Shanghai in just sixty-two days—the fastest passage of the season. His first letter to Hitty from Shanghai is dated March 4, 1859:

*I am obliged to associate here with the big ship Captains for there is no small ones here. I find I can blow as well as any of them. We have made the best passage that has been* *made from Bangkok this season. Vessels have been 80 and 90 days. The Old Granada is up and dressed…Ships are loading for New York at $5.00 a ton, so you may judge times are hard; we used to get $4.00 from Baltimore to Boston.*

Captain Taylor worked into steady packet trips in the *Granada* between Shanghai and Nagasaki, carrying both freight and passengers, and he remained in this trade for more than six months. In February 1860, after he had been in China almost a year, Captain Taylor received staggering news. He heard in Shanghai that his employer, Howes & Co., had failed. He had just come back from Nagasaki.

*On my arrival here the first news that came to my ears was that Messrs. Howes & Company had failed and was broke down as flat as they could be…The news comes direct from Chatham, Captain Isaiah Hardy received a letter from his wife. I laid awake most all night thinking of it. I wish I was in the Western Country as far as I could get and [on] a small farm. Then I should not have to think of vessels or owners.*

Despite the news, he continued with packet runs as if all were well. It was a good thing he did, as the report turned out to be false. Captain Taylor capitalized on some trouble between imperialists and rebels in Shanghai by chartering the *Granada* to a group of Chinese merchants to store their possessions aboard while the hostilities lasted. Their tab came to $1,200. Also, business began to be brisk. On his last trip to Nagasaki he had made $12,600. The Japanese packet runs ended by December 1860, so he returned to coasting again out of Shanghai.

In March 1861 the firm of Olyphant & Co. chartered the *Granada* and its master for a trip up the Yangtse-Kiang River to Nanking. This was the captain's first experience in river work and he had the distinction of being the first American to take a merchant vessel to Nanking. After several months taking the *Granada* between Shanghai and Nanking, Olyphant & Co. sent Captain Taylor back to New York to superintend the building of a new steamer, which he would bring back to China for the river run. After more than three and a half years, husband Simeon finally was bound for home!

While this new vessel was being built, the company asked Captain Taylor to go to Montevideo in the spring of 1862. There, he was to take another of its steamers, the *Mississippi*,[2] out to China and then return in time to put the finishing touches on the new vessel. He took Hitty, then pregnant with daughter Maria, and thirteen-year-old Emma with him. In a fierce August storm, the vessel took on water, and although there were five pumps, they were inadequate to keep the ship afloat. All had to abandon ship. Passengers and crew were transferred to the British brig *Minstrel* and the Swedish bark *Prins Oscar*. Captain Taylor and his family got to St. Helena, an island in the South Atlantic, in September. By November they were back in New York. Olyphant & Co.'s new vessel was not yet complete and Captain Simeon was able to vacation at home in Chatham until September 1863.

The new steamer, christened *Kin Kiang*, was launched in September 1863 to go to China. The first letter Hitty received was from St. Vincent in the Grenadines written in

Simeon's droll manner: "The Island of St. Vincent I should think was the last place in the world, and there was not enough left to finish it."

He was keeping a lookout for the infamous Confederate raider, the *Alabama*, which was plundering any Union vessel she could find. His new ship was lucky on her maiden voyage and did not fall victim to the marauder. The captain reached Shanghai in the middle of May 1864 and immediately went to work on the river, running the *Kin Kiang* between Shanghai and Hankow, a trip of about ten days. Two of his brothers—Horace and Prince, both shipmasters—were also in the Orient. He wrote to Hitty:

> *Horace is down the Sea again somewhere. I have not heard from him lately. I understand that Horace is in Shanghai waiting for the bark* Wild Rover. *He has sold the* Young Greek *and is going to take charge of the* W.R. [Wild Rover].

Prince had gone to Japan to recover from a bout of dysentery. That is where he met with Neesima Shimeta, a young Japanese of the samurai class, who later was brought to Chatham by his brother, Captain Horace Taylor. (See Captain Horace Taylor's profile, which follows.)

By the end of 1864, the captain was feeling prosperous. "Only think, Hitty," he wrote, "my wages have been raised to $250 per month." In another letter, he spoke again of their good fortune.

> *I think we both ought to be pretty well satisfied…you being high cockalorum of your mansion and me the same of a fine steam ship during the hard times and troubles in our country.*

He continued to run the *Kin Kiang* as a river packet between Shanghai and Hankow until the fall of 1865 when Olyphant & Co. sold her to Russell & Co. It was the latter company's intent to make daily trips up the Canton River between Hong Kong and Canton. Captain Taylor stayed with the *Kin Kiang* and took her to Hong Kong. A letter to Hitty is a lively account of the run and his new arrangement:

> *Canton, December 16, 1865. We left Shanghai on the 3rd of this month and made the run to Hong Kong in 58 hours, the best time that ever was made, and there was quite an excitement about it…It was very pleasing to Messrs Russell & Co. I was taken by the hand at once and must go and dine with the head of the House, and they think that the* Kin Kiang *and the Captain are all right. The business of running on the Canton river is much better than the Yang Tse; we depart at 9:00 A.M. and arrive at 2:00 P.M. every day…We have strong opposition, but the old* Kin Kiang *can beat them all. The* Fire Dart *is our opponent. We can and do beat her one half hour on the passage easy. This afternoon I think there was 1,000 people on the dock to see us. [When we] came in, gave us three cheers as we came alongside the dock. I tell you Hitty, there is some pleasure in having a fast boat and more pleasure to have business you like.*

In writing to her husband during 1865, Mehitable apprised him of what was taking place at home regarding his fellow sea captains:

> *Saw Captain Adolphus Ryder. He told me he thought he should try to get his living on land; he intends to try his luck in Chicago. It is very dull in regards to Captains getting business. Captain David Harding says, "Tell Sim to come home and go out West with him in the pork business or keeping hotel." Capt. Ryder has gone to Chicago and gone into the fish business. Captain Stephen Bearse has gone into the boot and shoe business in Boston.*

In April 1866, Captain Taylor resigned his command of the *Kin Kiang* but agreed to make one more voyage for Russell & Co., taking the steamer *Plymouth Rock* to Shanghai. Early in the summer, he took passage for home. So ended the sea exploits of Captain Simeon N. Taylor and began the retail life of Mr. Simeon Taylor. His career change was made soon after his return from China. A letter to Hitty from Roxbury, Massachusetts, on June 8, 1867, sounds like his old self: upbeat, excited and enthusiastic.

> *I think we have got a first rate location for Business. We have sold a little over $900.00 since I arrived…we of course cannot tell just what percentage we have made as we bought every thing for so much money and have not had time to take account of stock. Every* [one] *tells us here that this is the best location in Roxbury for Business…We haven't got our cards out neither have we our Shingle yet but expect to soon. It will read something like this Taylor & Howes Successors to Calvin Bird…*
> *I wrote to Em* [their daughter Emma] *that she might have a silk dress and could pay as high as $2.50 per yd…What do the folks say about my going with the Furniture Business…I suppose they talk some…let them talk. Tell Washington[3] when he comes to Boston to come and see me. I want him to give me a few lessons in trading…I am in the store writing this. I send you all lots of my love.*

Simeon Taylor, shopkeeper, was becoming restless without a house in Roxbury and his dear wife to adorn it, as we read in his letter to her, which is dated June 21, 1867:

> *My dear Hitty,*
> *Keep your tea warm. Tomorrow evening I may take it into my head to come to Chatham. I have not decided yet. Monday will be a holiday in this city as the President expects to be about. Saturday is rather a busy day with us however I shall try to leave if possible. I wish we were living in Roxbury then I would be at home. I think I shall try to sell our house the first opportunity…will you agree to it. You can tell me when I come home. I shall not go to meeting Sunday. My coat is rather dusty. You may look for me. Your Hub, Sim*

Shopkeeper Simeon scouted the market for suitable houses, finally finding one that he was sure Mehitable would like. According to his letter of July 22, he seemed to have found one he liked:

*The house is new and finished in good style with a cellar and the whole bigness of the house and a large furnace to heate all the rooms except the Kitchen . . . I think you would like it first rate. The house is 2½ story 4 good chambers finished in good style. Now write me what I had better do or come and see it your self.*

And then he "turned the screw" by adding plaintively, "I am sleeping in the store yet." He was hoping, no doubt, to get some immediate, positive response. By July 28, the deed was done and in his letter to Hitty he admonished her not to get too "excited over it and get sick. If you can get anyone to help you do so and take it coolly for if we are two or three weeks it matters not. I will say the rest another time."

There aren't any further notes on what had to be done so we are not privy to all the details—the new paper to be hung throughout the new house at 5 Tolman Place, Boston Highlands, or the packing for the move from Chatham. It all took place, and by 1872 there was a card, in a scrapbook kept by youngest daughter Maria:

*Mr. and Mrs. S.N. Taylor*
*Receive Friends*
*At the Marriage of their Daughter*
*Emma H. Taylor*
*and*
*George H. Munroe*
*Wednesday Evening, October 30, 1872*
*5 Tolman Place, Highlands at 8 o'clock*

Captain Simeon's land-based exploits over the next two decades aren't known. There are reports that he was in the fish business, traveling to the Midwest to take orders for salt cod. What we do know is that Captain Taylor died on November 8, 1898, after having been happily married to his dear Hitty for a full fifty years. He was seventy-two years old. He and his wife and children are buried in People's Cemetery, Chatham.

# ZENAS NICKERSON JR.
## (1827–1894)
### *A Victim of the* Velma

Captain Zenas Nickerson Jr. is inextricably associated with the demise of the bark *Velma*, of which he was master, when she was wrecked off Plymouth, Massachusetts, in January 1867. It seems unfair that we remember a tragedy as the most prominent thing about his life. That the disaster was unavoidable and Captain Zenas's actions heroic will be apparent.

Captain Zenas Jr. had a good teacher and model in becoming a master mariner—his father, who was also a sea captain. An early command in 1857 was the bark *Helen Maria*, a coasting vessel owned largely by Richard Taylor, according to *Queens of the Western Ocean* by Carl C. Cutler. She was listed in the New York Shipping Register, too. These notations speak to the period of the Civil War when the *Helen Maria* undoubtedly was carrying freight and supplies needed for the war. Captain Zenas bought into her as did others in Chatham

A note that has survived mentions that our good captain was also owner of the bark *Horace Scudder*, which was built in 1864 and sailed out of Boston. Our research says the bark also was engaged in coastal commerce going up and down the Atlantic shore. In 1867, Captain Zenas was in command of the bark *Velma* and was sailing farther afield.

There are at least two records of the wreck of the *Velma*, which took place January 17, 1867. The most complete report was by Professor Carol Wight, who wrote *The Wreck of the* Velma.[1] We will let him tell the story:

> The bark Velma, *captained by Zenas Nickerson of Chatham left Smyrna with a load of wood, canary food, boxwood, figs and raisins on October 20th, 1866, bound for Boston. The first night her mainsail was carried away and she sprung her fore topsail yard in a gale. Of her subsequent trip through the Mediterranean and what ports she touched at, if any, we have no record, we are told that she had a fairly good passage across the Western Ocean.*[2]

Professor Carol Wight's story of the wreck of the *Velma* begins with a Latin quotation: "It is necessary to navigate; it is not necessary to live." The *Velma*'s captain was Zenas Nickerson. *Courtesy of the Chatham (MA) Historical Society, Inc.*

*January 17, 1867 at about 4 a.m. she made Cape Cod Light, bearing west by north about 12 miles distant. The wind freshened from the southeast and they hauled the vessel by the wind and shortened sail. At about 2 p.m. the wind hauled to east northeast increasing steadily with very heavy snow, the bark was suddenly thrown on her beam ends. By then the decks were full of water, ice and snow, and the vessel was unmanageable and drifted across Massachusetts Bay helplessly, though some 10 tons of figs were got out of the hatches and thrown overboard, which did not help matters much.*

*All standing and running rigging below the top sail yards was sheathed in ice, the snow flying in clouds, the air bitterly keen. It was impossible to tack or ware with the ice locked rigging. Soundings were futile, observations out of the question. The storm from contemporary accounts was a record breaker…*

*At 2 o'clock Saturday morning, then, the* Velma *struck half a mile off shore and breaking over the ledge, she came within 20 rods off Manomet Beach and then swung round with her head to the sea, presumably pointing northeast. The first sea that boarded her shattered her skylight. The next flooded her and put out the fire. All hands who had been ordered by Captain Nickerson to come aft and gather round the stove to keep from freezing, were now driven on deck. The boats were blocks of ice and could not be launched. The main and poop decks were flooded by every sea that came aboard and nearly every sea came aboard, while the vessel pounded heavily and was beginning to head off shore. The men had taken to the lee rigging which was landward and was from both these circumstances the quarter any help would come. The captain had seen to it that the men were dressed with all they had in any of clothes, one man having on half a dozen sets of underwear and another four pairs of socks. This, of course, would not keep a man dry, but it would check heat radiation and consequent freezing. The cook, William Simpson of England, who from the nature of his job, was possessed of less apparel than the rest of the crew, was encased in the captain's best overcoat and this little detail shows clearly that though Captain Zenas Nickerson's discipline may have been of the iron variety, the man's inmost heart never went off the gold standard.*

*The cook's station in the rigging was the least favorable and he was under an almost continuous shower of spray, that froze as it struck him. He had unusually long hair and thick at that. This caught the driving spray and sleet so that his locks like those of Absolom proved fatal, for his head became at last completely encased in ice so that it looked to Captain Zenas like a big frozen water bucket. Early in the morning the unfortunate man could no longer hold on and fell, striking in his fall Manuel Guestres, one of the crew from the Western Islands and both men were swept into the sea.*

*The others were all saved, that is Captain Zenas Nickerson and First Mate, Starks Lewis Nickerson, both of Chatham, Second Mate John G. Allen of New Bedford, and of the crew, Augustus L. Jenkins of Portsmouth, N.H., John Florida of N.Y., John Perry of Lisbon and Joseph Silva* [also known as Joseph Manta] *of Boston...*

*The rescue was hazardous. Seven men of Plymouth, Henry B. Holmes, Robert Bearay, J.B. Bartlett, Octavious Reany, James R. Lynch, C.W. Holmes and L.R. Briggs launched the Humane Society boat, which was thrown back on the shore rocks and stove full of holes. These were plugged with clothing and she was successfully launched and cleared the surf, though she had to be bailed to keep afloat. When they reached the* Velma *no line could be thrown out for some time for the running rigging was a tangled mess of hemp and ice.*

*Mr. Howard, the Second Mate* [in the rescue boat] *was nearly lost. He had been of the first to weaken and was in charge of Joseph Manta, but he fell into the sea when going over into the lifeboat. He was saved however and all were landed and taken to the Manomet House. Here Dr. Alexander Jackson of Plymouth and Dr. C.J. Wood of Chiltonville...attended them and as one account states, performed a number of necessary amputations...*

*The responsibilities of Captain Nickerson did not end here. News of the wreck had to be got through to the owners of the* Velma *and the consignees of her cargo in Boston by sleigh, which was furnished by Mr. Chandler, the hotel proprietor. The horses were hitched tandem with a little horse in front...On top of the hardship and exposure of the wreck, a chilly trip like this was very hazardous to say the least, but Captain Zenas deemed it his duty and did it successfully...*

*As to the fate of the bark and her cargo the statement of the adjusters will suffice: "the cargo was nearly all saved by Lighters in a badly damaged condition and the wreck of the vessel was sold at auction for the benefit of all concerned."*

The *Velma* was a bark of 340 tons, built in East Boston by Paul Curtis for Captain Nickerson's command. Her owners were Baker, Morrell, Ryder and Hardy of Boston, and Captain Nickerson acquired an interest in her himself. She was a handsome vessel, as proven by her picture, which was painted by an artist from Smyrna and is owned by the captain's son, George Nickerson II. Professor Wight notes the ship was named *Velma* after the daughter of the builder, and Captain Nickerson's daughter, Velma Nickerson, was named after the bark.

Wight shows how Yankee tact was needed in handling the crew in this story. George Nickerson asked one of the crew whom he met years after if he was on Mr. Nickerson's watch. "No," was the answer, "I was in Mr. Lewis's watch. He was our First Mate." Mr. Lewis was Starks Lewis Nickerson, Captain Zenas's brother. However, the crew knew him only as Mr. Lewis. "This piece of innocent state-craft rendered government matters more easy and did not over emphasize…the preeminence of the family," Professor Wight reminds us.

Ships like the *Velma* were built for the coasting trade, running between Boston and Baltimore and other East Coast ports. When crowded out by steamers, these ships took to "blue water" and European or even Far Eastern ports. They were generally owned in shares, the captain often holding a tenth. Depending upon the captain's character and ability, his presence served as an inducement for fellow townsmen to buy a share or two themselves.

Captain Zenas had married Mary Ann Taylor, daughter of Ephraim Taylor, in 1849. They had six children—George II, Zenas A., Mary Ann, Velma, Priscilla and Geneve. Following the loss of the *Velma*, Zenas retired from the sea. His health had suffered greatly from the exposure and he had internal injuries. He went into the grocery and grain business, adding the sale of coal, too.

Wight explains:

> *Captain Nickerson's coal, grain, hay and supplies came by water and J.H. Tripp & Co. conducted a business of their own on Harding's Beach. Vessels anchored wherever there was anchorage ground and Zenas's venture prospered. He not only fitted out and supplied weirs but bought into some of the vessels and this held their trade and yielded a profit.*

Captain Zenas died October 22, 1894, and was buried in the Union Cemetery. His business lived on under the name of Zenas Nickerson's Sons for many years.

# Jonathan B. Atkins
## (1828–1899)
### *Sailing to the "Down Under"*

A North Chatham family treasures a cup and saucer—souvenir china featuring a painting of the bark *Daniel Webster* when she was under the command of Captain Jonathan B. Atkins. Captain Atkins was all of twenty-six years old when he became its master. It was his first command and one that lasted four years.

His second vessel was another bark, the *Sachem,* of which he became skipper in the fall of 1858. The *Sachem* was built by Silvanus Smith in Boston and launched in 1858 at a cost of $29,915.80, outfitted.

With Captain Atkins at the helm, she left Boston in November 1858 destined for Honolulu. She arrived there in April 1859. No sooner than that voyage was completed, the bark returned to Boston—this time carrying, among other things, sisal, pineapples and other fruit. As was customary, the *Sachem* settled accounts and paid her stockholders upon return to Boston. Since we have few reports of such settlements, it is interesting to see what the vessel earned for its stockholders on the Honolulu voyage: Captain Jonathan's father, Zenas, was the primary shareholder with fourteen sixty-fourths of shares, and on this voyage his earnings amounted to $1,059.75. E.H. Ryder, with six sixty-fourths, earned $454.19. Those who owned four sixty-fourths, including the captain himself, earned $302.76. As captain, Jonathan also earned master's wages, plus a percentage of the cargo value. The shareholders with just one sixty-fourth, earned the handsome sum of $75.69 on this voyage.

After *Sachem*'s initial voyage, there follows a dizzying series of trips taken by Captain Jonathan to ports that included Genoa, Italy; Cagliari, Sardinia; New South Wales; Sidney, Australia; and Valparaiso, Chile. The *Sachem* regularly sailed from Boston to Melbourne, Australia.

By June 1863, Captain Jonathan was master of yet a fourth vessel, the *Arica*, which he took to Pensacola, New Orleans, and back to Boston. The *Arica* also sailed from Cadiz to New York. Other voyages took the captain and the *Arica* as far afield as Cronstadt, off

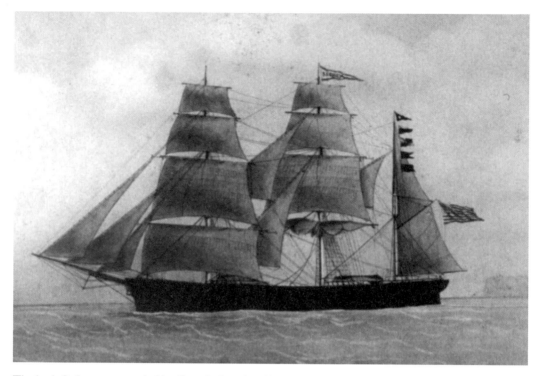

The bark *Sachem*, commanded by Captain Jonathan B. Atkins, made a whirlwind world tour, visiting Italy, Sardinia, Chile, New Zealand and Australia. *Courtesy, The Chatham (MA) Historical Society, Inc.*

St. Petersburg; New Orleans; Le Havre, France; and Guttenborg, Sweden—she always returned to Boston. Since all this activity falls within the Civil War period, it seems probable that the *Arica* was carrying British registry, considering England was neutral. A memo noting the *Arica* was insured by "Lloyds in the amount of $30.00" adds weight to the theory.

The log of the bark *Sarah* out of Boston notes the captain was in command in June 1867.

The captain enjoyed a close, warm relationship with his sister, Rhoda. These letters to her date from 1869 to 1880 and relate a great deal about his business as well as his state of mind.

*March 1869, San Francisco: My dear Sister, We had a very moderate and pleasant passage out but tedious and I found myself very lonesome indeed. We are now loading for Cork for orders. Shall probably be ordered to Liverpool or London. Expect to sail about the 5th. Please write me in Liverpool, care of Warner & Barson, Bark Sarah. From your loving brother, J.B. Atkins.*

*August 24, 1869, Liverpool: I could find no business to come home with so I have bought a cargo of coal and salt on owners' account and shall proceed to San Francisco. Sorry* to hear our cousin Joshua had met with an accident…Please send me two copies of the "Era" to San Francisco, care of J.W.H. Campbell. We expect to start in about ten days. Brother Jonathan.

December 22, 1871, Dunedin, New Zealand: My dear sister Rhoda, I am quite disappointed in not receiving any letter from you since our father's death…One of the mail steamers was lost with all her mails and I presume your letters were there. All letters for Australia or New Zealand should be marked San Francisco. I miss father's letters very much. It is hard to think that I can never have any more from him or see him again…I wrote in my last if Mother wishes advice I thought she would do well to call on Mr. Bea but just as you all think best. I wrote to Capt. Gustavus Ryder by the last mail to advise you about insurance on the Sarah that was to insure her for the passage home only which is for the best way at present.

We arrived here on the 1st—twelve days from Melbourne. Are now loading wool for Boston. Hope to get away early in February with a good freight if all goes well and we are spared. I hope to be home in May next. Sarah [Jonathan's wife] has been quite ill since our arrival but is now getting better. Trust she will soon be all right again.

Summer is now commencing here and the weather is very pleasant indeed. They have flowers here in great profusion, fruits and vegetables are just now on the market. Upon the whole I think New Zealand is a very fine country at this season. The mail leaves here for America via San Francisco on the 22nd of every month…Wishing you all a Merry Christmas and very happy New Year. With much love to all I remain your ever loving and affectionate Brother Jonathan.

January 1873, Adelaide: Yours received at Melbourne…Had a long and tedious passage out to Melbourne…Our stay at Melbourne was somewhat prolonged on account of the Christmas Holidays which lasted nearly 2 weeks…Had a fine run of two days to this port and are now loading cargo wheat for Liverpool, expect to sail about the 1st of the month. They have no rain here at this season and almost a cloudless sky and at times the heat and dust almost unbearable…J.B.A."

March 16, 1875, Antofagasta: I don't know that you know exactly where Antofagasta is; it is a small seaport in Bolivia about 500 miles north of Valparaiso. It is just on the Tropic of Capricorn and a most miserable place…not a sign of vegetation for many hundred miles around, nothing but a sandy desert, no fresh water only what is condensed. It never rains here and the weather is always fine, for the last two months we have not had a drop of rain but continual fine weather…thermometer steady at about seventy degrees. Must say the climate is delightful but give [me] old New England with all its changes. We are now loaded and expect to sail tomorrow for Philadelphia…hope with God's blessing to reach there last of June or first of…J.B.A.

October 1877, Freeport Mills: My dear sister, On arrival at Port Townsend found business very dull. After waiting some time were enabled to secure low freight of lumber *to west coast of South America—are now loading at Freeport Mills about 35 miles above Port Townsend. Not much of a place. No others live here but Mill hands. Just across the bay about 2 miles is the very thriving town of Seattle, quite a smart place for these parts. I like this part of the country very much the climate fine much better than with us none of those great extremes of heat and cold. And all the necessarys of life abound. Plenty of fruit and lots of salmon cheap, we buy them off the Indians for 3 cents apiece weighing from 5 to 6 pounds, plenty of clams and flat fish, so we live nicely if times is dull. Fresh beef fine quality four cents a pound but I wont say anymore in that direction for fear that you will want to take a husband and emigrate. The people here seem to be very healthy and hospitable but in many cases rather rough as in all new countrys that element is apt to predominate. Indians are very plenty about here but very peaceful and quiet. We expect to be loaded about the 20^{th}…I had a few rare plants from Japan but gave them away as they were likely to die on the vessel and I saw no chance to get them home. With much love, Your ever loving brother Jonathan.*

*February 17, 1880, New Orleans: Found the* Sarah *here all right, it seems quite like getting home again…Sarah [his wife] seems to be quite taken with New Orleans… Business is very dull here, nothing in view yet. Shall no doubt go to some part of Europe. I enjoyed my visit home very much with nothing to do I should not be content much longer. Would rather go to sea in a good vessel than be on shore and as going to sea seems to be my natural calling, think I shall be content to go a while longer. Jon.*

*P.S. Have chartered for Havre cargo cotton expect to get away about 10^{th} March. J.B.A.*

In the spring of 1883, a newspaper entry notes:

*We understand Capt. Jonathan Atkins will stop at home during the next voyage of his vessel, bark* Sarah. *Captain Judson Doane of West Chatham takes her on the next trip to Australia.*

That was a decision that Captain Jonathan must have agonized over later, for Captain Doane was his good friend. Three weeks before the *Sarah*'s expected arrival in Australia, the bark under Doane's command encountered a storm. Heavy seas broke over the vessel during the storm. Afterward, four feet of water were found in the cabin where Mrs. Doane, who had accompanied her husband on the voyage, was found dead.

There is no indication exactly when Captain Atkins ceased going to sea, but in 1894 he paid five hundred dollars for a lot with a house and outbuildings on Cross Street, Chatham. The report notes he and his wife were planning a move home to Chatham after a sojourn in Medford.

Captain Jonathan and his wife, Sarah (Eldredge) Atkins, whom he had married in 1847, had only one child, a daughter, who died in infancy. Mrs. Atkins sailed with her husband, as noted from his letters. Jonathan died of Bright's disease in 1899. Both he and Sarah are interred in Chatham's Union Cemetery.

# GRACE BROS & C.°

W. R. GRACE & Co.
New-York.

## CALLAO & LIMA

J. W. GRACE & Co.
San Francisco

## GRACE & Co.
### VALPARAISO.

*This Charter Party,* made and concluded in the City of this *Lima, this Twelfth day of February 1885 Between J. B. Atkins, Master of the of Am⁵ bark the "Sarah" of Boston of 661 Reg. tons. and classed ⅔ I. 1. 1. now at anchor in Callao Bay of the first part, and Grace Bros & C° of the second part.*

*Witnesseth,* that the said party of the first part, in consideration of the covenants and agreements hereinafter mentioned, to be kept and performed by the said party of the second part, doth conve-, nant and agree on the freighting and chartering of the said vessel unto the said party of the second part. for a voyage from ~~the port of~~ *a mill or loading port in Puget Sound or Burrard Inlet to Callao, direct. The vessel to proceed at once to Royal Roads or Port Townsend where orders as to loading port will be given by Messrs. J. W. Grace & agents within 48 hours of telegraphic advice of arrival having been received by Messrs. J. W. Grace & C° Sundays excepted.*

on the terms following, that is to say:

FIRST. — The said party of the first part doth engage that the said vessel, in and during the said voyage, shall be kept tight, staunch, well-fitted, tackled and provided with every requisite, and with men and provisions necessary for such voyage.

SECOND. — The said party of the first part, doth further engage, that the whole of the said vessel (with the exception of the cabin, ~~the deck~~ and the necessary room for the accommodation of the crew, and of the sails, cables and provisions) shall be at the sole use and disposal of the said party of the second part, during the voyage aforesaid.

THIRD. — The said party of the first part doth further engage to take and receive on board the said vessel during the aforesaid voyage, all such lawful goods and merchandise as the said party of the second part, or his agent, may think proper to ship.

Grace Bros. & Co. chartered Captain J.B. Atkins's bark *Sarah* "at anchor in Callao Bay" for a voyage to Puget Sound. The document is dated February 12, 1885, Lima, Peru. No cargo is mentioned. *Joseph A. Nickerson Jr. Collection.*

# HORACE S. TAYLOR
## (1829–1869)
### Brought Neesima Shimeta to U.S.

C aptain Horace S. Taylor is in the history books because he was master of the bark *Wild Rover*, which brought Neesima Shimeta from Shanghai to Boston in 1865, and thence to Chatham. Neesima Shimeta, a young samurai-class Japanese man of twenty-one years, had fled Japan because he wanted to embrace Christianity and, through it, to see needed reforms brought about in his country.

Neesima made his way out of Japan,[1] and eventually reached Shanghai where he had the good fortune to board the *Wild Rover*. He had no money but Captain Taylor agreed to have him as cabin boy on the trip. The captain wasn't able to pronounce his name and so called him "Joe," the name he took with him to America. Later he added "Hardy" as a middle name—for Alpheus Hardy, owner of the *Wild Rover*—and so became Joseph Hardy Neesima.

Mr. and Mrs. Hardy saw to his education at Philips Academy, Amherst College and Andover Seminary, from which he graduated in 1870. He returned to Japan and founded Doshisha University, which began with six students. Today its student body is upwards of thirty-five thousand. Representatives of the university have visited the Atwood House Museum several times—the last in the fall of 2005—to see the artifacts and photos of Neesima with the Taylor family and the *Wild Rover* painting that hangs in the Atkins-Kent China Trade Gallery.

Let us return to our Captain Horace Scudder Taylor. He married Corrinda Atkins in May 1852—the daughter of Zenas and Rhoda Atkins. Corrinda had a brother Jonathan (see previous profile) and a sister Rhoda. Corrinda and Rhoda were devoted to each other and were faithful letter writers. Their letters give us an intimate glimpse into the times and voyages of both the Taylor and Atkins family members. In a letter from Corrinda to her sister Rhoda on May 21, 1855, she wrote:

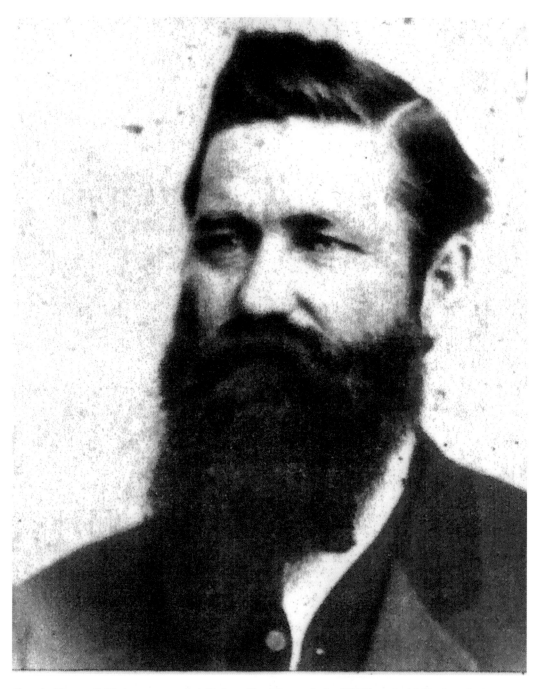

Captain Horace S. Taylor commanded Alpheus Hardy's vessel, the *Wild Rover*, in 1865 when she brought a young Japanese man the captain called Joe to America. *Joseph A. Nickerson, Jr. Collection.*

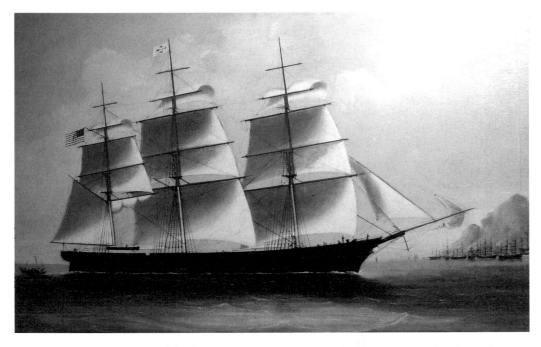

The ship *Wild Rover* brought Neesima Shimeta to Boston to "embrace Christianity" and to learn about America so he could bring needed reforms back to his country. *Joseph A. Nickerson, Jr. Collection.*

*You have probably heard of our safe arrival here* [Boston] *and may be looking for me home. I want to come very much but I want to stop until Horace finds out where he is going and I can not tell when that will be…We have had a much better passage home than out. Plenty of head winds and calms though I was not as sick as I was going out and am now in very good health and hear that you all are at home.* [Brother] *Jonathan is very well. He went to Barnstable Saturday and came back this morning. Found Sarah* [Captain Atkins's wife] *much better than when he went away. She could write and sew a little.*

*I was sorry I did not get your letter in Palermo but I can get your dress here if you want me to. I should like to know what style you would like figured or plaid and what color. Horace has just put some oranges and lemons on board Capt. Smith's packet. They are marked Capt. John Taylor. Half are for them. Try to get them as soon as the packet comes as they may rot if kept on board.*

*Simeon* [Corrinda's brother-in-law] *and Mehitable have been on board and I have asked all the questions about the folks in Chatham that I could think of. Emma* [their little daughter] *is very smart she staid with us Saturday night, her father and mother were gone to E. Boston. Be sure and write as soon as you get this. I forgot to say that I do not hardly think I shall go the next voyage. C.*

Following is another letter from Corrinda Taylor to her sister, Rhoda, written from Boston on December 7, 1856:

*Dear sister,…The lamps I shall not get as I am not very fond of going on Chatham St. and enquiring after gentlemen…The cloak cost $18.00 and the bonnet $6.50…I have bought a set of furs for $14.00…Horace has not yet decided about what he will do. The vessel is not chartered yet. Capt. Taylor* [Richard Taylor, Horace's employer] *does not seem to want him to stop. Says if he* [Horace] *goes I must go too…*

Another letter from Corrinda to her sister seems to follow the one above by just a few days. She *was* going with her husband after all.

*We are going down the harbor with a fine wind and shall soon be off at sea. I have sent a carpetbag of things by Capt. R. Taylor for the ones whose names you will find on them. I hope your skirts will suit you. Please forward the other things and write me in Malta if they switch especially Mary's. Tell Rebecca I tried every store on Hanover St. for her silk and could not* [find] *any this shade. At least I found these few skeins on Tremont Row all they had…I gave 19 cents for this will keep the other change she gave me till I get back. It has been stormy two days which prevented me from going out as I should have done had it been pleasant. The carpetbag is for Mother. I hope it will suit her. Write to Malta after we are gone two or three weeks…write all the news. Horace is not very well. I felt afraid yesterday he was really going to be sick but he is better today.*

*Direct letters to American Consul Malta. We expect to go to Smyrna* [Greece] *from there. I shall want to hear from you all when we get there. Was rather disappointed in not meeting father here. Tell Ellen I will try to keep the journal for her, and Alvin must be good. I do not know as my things are left as they should be, I came in such a hurry…I meant to have written Mehitable but shall have to wait till we get out* [at sea] *I did hope Simeon would arrive before we left but he has not come yet.*

*Horace has left a letter and notes at Ryder & Hardy's for father if he should come to Boston. If he does not they will send them down to him. Capt. R. Taylor will also pay to him the earnings of the Western Sea. Horace was in hopes to have seen him* [Corrinda's father] *as he wanted to pay him house rent but if anything should happen to us he will probably have enough in his hands to make him whole.*

*I like the appearance of the passenger very much, wish there was one or two ladies going then I should have someone but men to see…tell Mother not to work to hard, I shall feel worried about her all the time as she does not seem very well…The pilot is to leave soon and I shall have to close this. Good bye from Corrinda.*

From Cape Coast Castle, West Coast Africa, on August 10, 1857 Corrinda wrote to her sister, in part:

*We have all enjoyed pretty good health since we have been here…Captain Elliot of Provincetown has died since we have been on the coast and some English Captain, but the English are very dissipated here which I think is the cause of their sickness. The coast is considered to be quite healthy if one takes proper care of themselves. We have been much longer in getting a homeward cargo than we expected to be, and had not an English*

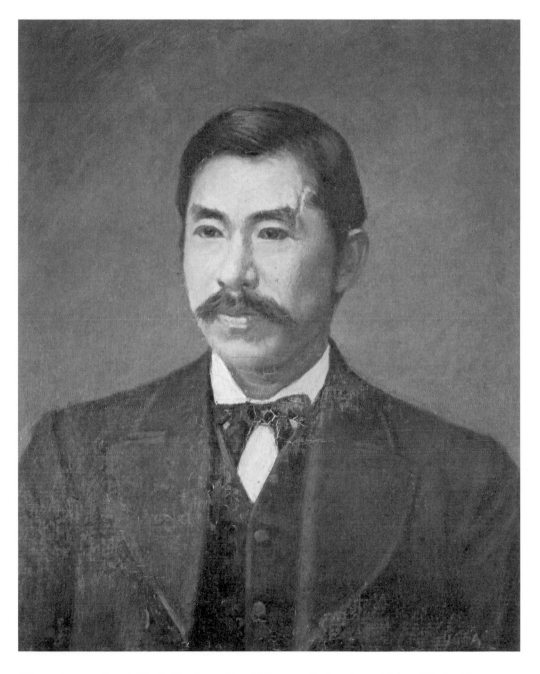

Shimeta became Joseph Hardy Neesima—his middle name for benefactor Alpheus Hardy. After attending Philips Academy, Amherst and Andover Seminary, he was ordained, returned to Japan to teach Christianity and founded Doshisha University there. *Joseph A. Nickerson, Jr. Collection.*

*Barque put in here in distress and obliged to sell her cargo of Palm Oil we should not have left in two months longer, so what was unfortunate for the English Bq. was very fortunate for us.*

*The Barque* Neopolitan, *Capt. David Ellis of Harwich arrived at Elmina* [8 miles away] *yesterday. He is to come to this place today and we are in hope to see him and possibly hear some news from home. We shall leave sometime this week, I think, and hope not to be over 50 or 60 days on the passage home…Yours affectionately, C.A. Taylor*

A letter, written while they were homeward bound on September 9, 1857, was most likely Corrinda's last. She died of yellow fever and was buried at sea. She was only twenty-six years old. Captain Taylor married a second time to Sophie Dodge, with whom he had an infant son who survived just a few months. No local records of either the date of the marriage, the birth of the child or of Sophie's death could be found.

There is a painting in the Peabody Museum of the *Bark* Western Sea *of Boston, Captain H. Taylor, leaving Marseilles, February 1859.* This captaincy was a part of a long and satisfying connection with the owner of the *Wild Rover*, Alpheus Hardy of Boston, who also hailed from Chatham. Captain Horace commanded the *Wild Rover* in 1855, 1856 and again from 1862 on. (Captain Benajah Crowell was master of the *Wild Rover* from 1858 to 1862, as documented earlier.)

In the years between his *Wild Rover* commands, Captain Taylor was master of the bark *Young Greek*[2] on a voyage to Valparaiso-Caldera, Chile, thence to New York in 1859. It was in 1864 that Captain Horace Taylor had brought the *Young Greek* to Shanghai on instructions to sell her. He waited there for his brother Simeon to arrive with the *Wild Rover*, which Captain Horace was to bring back home. It was that trip back to the States that had Neesima on board as cabin boy. In addition to this unusual passenger, the ship carried a full cargo of hemp from Manila for Boston. When she was ready to sail out of Manila there was a report that a Confederate marauder was lying in wait for U.S. vessels at the entrance of the harbor. The mates busied themselves with preparations for defense, but no action was necessary and the *Rover* passed without incident. They left Manila on April 1, 1865, and reached Boston four months later. When they reached Cape Cod, a fisherman told them that the Civil War was ended and President Lincoln had been assassinated.

Another trip on the *Rover* in 1868 from New York to San Francisco in 132 days—an unheard of time for any sailing vessel to travel that distance, all the way around Cape Horn and so far north—provides a measure of the captain's mettle. Captain Horace Taylor had circumnavigated the globe twice. And at forty years of age, he was still a young man by all standards when, in December 1869, in crossing on a ferry from Boston to East Boston he attempted to step ashore before the boat had been secured. He slipped and fell between the boat and the dock and was crushed. He lived only a few minutes. He was eulogized as "a man held in high esteem and confidence by those in whose company he sailed." He is buried in Chatham's Union Cemetery.

# John E. Mallowes
## (1830–1864)
### Died in 1864 Gale

Captain John Mallowes was the older brother of Captain Benjamin Mallowes Jr., and both were sons of Captain Benjamin Mallowes of Chatham. John began his work at sea on barges, notably the barge *Alice*, plus several others. However, he soon decided to get his master's license and follow in the footsteps of his father and other Mallowes men by commanding deep-sea fishing vessels.

Captain John was the victim of one of the most horrendous gales ever recorded on Nova Scotia's Grand Banks. He was master of the schooner *Emma Frances*, with a crew of eight men, seven from Chatham and another man whose hometown was not known. An account of the loss of the schooner *Emma Frances* follows as was recorded in *The Fishermen's Memorial and Record Book* by George H. Proctor in 1873:

> *1864 was another disastrous year to the fishermen, proving, with the exception of 1862, the most unfortunate year since the Georges' [Georges Banks] fisheries commenced. By these sad disasters to the fishing fleet, eighty-five men found a watery grave, and thirteen men were lost, viz: eight [vessels] on Georges, two in the bay of St. Lawrence, two in the Newfoundland fishing and one in the freighting business.*
>
> *The night of March 22ⁿᵈ will be long remembered as the commencement of a severe northeaster. There were at this time about 100 sail on Georges, and the howling of the wind carried sad forebodings to many anxious wives, mothers, and other near and dear friends of the Georges men. They knew full well that nothing short of a miracle would bring all of that fleet back to port, and the dread question, "who will be lost?" repeated itself over and over again in the minds of the anxious watchers here at home. It was a solemn time, and all hearts felt that there were to be lamentations for those who would never return; and finally, when one by one, these Georges men came creeping back to port, and days and weeks passed in anxious hope*

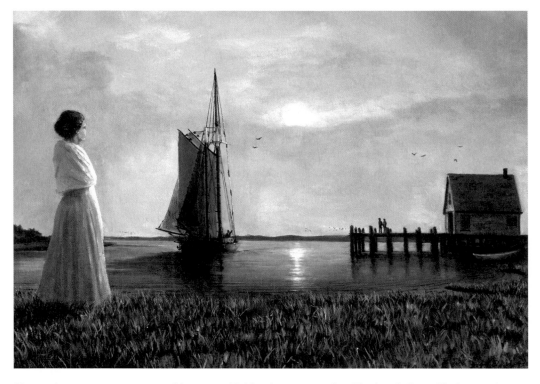

*Homecoming* portrays a woman waiting to see if this schooner entering Chatham's Stage Harbor carries her loved ones. Captain John Mallowes sailed a similar vessel to Georges Banks, but in 1864 he never returned home. *Painting by Jeff Eldredge.*

*that others would follow, it was found that six Chatham vessels were missing, as follows:*

*Schooner* John G. Dennis, *ten men*
*Schooner* Light of Home, *nine men*
*Schooner* Oliver Burnham, *nine men*
*Schooner* Nawadaha, *ten men*
*Schooner* Emma Frances, *nine men*
*Schooner* R.E. Spofford, *ten men*

*All of the rescued men were loud in their praise of Captain Daniel Nalty [and] of the tug and its crew, and seafaring men here today were unanimous in declaring the captain's performance to be one of the most courageous and skillful in the annals of the sea. Upon his arrival his company extended him hearty thanks and congratulations.*

*The tug not only stood by the barges until all their men had been saved, but awaited all night in the mountainous seas until the last barge had gone under. Then the tug made for port.*

*One small life lost was that of the cat on the Barge* Helen. *The crew searched for her before they took to their life boat; but she could not be found. Peggy, the dog, however, was saved.*

*At 1 A.M., Captain John E. Mallowes of Roxbury and Chatham, in command, ordered his motorboat over the side and he and three men, Eric Ohman, engineer; Charles Rundlett, cook, and Edward Handrigan, deck hand, jumped aboard and started for the tug. Both craft tossed so in the terrific seas that jumping from one to the other was difficult and dangerous. The small boat had come but a few yards from the barge when a tremendous wave broke over her, half-filled her with water, and stopped her engine. The tug captain worked his way alongside and heaved lines to her, and just as the lines were made fast, another wave smashed the motor boat to kindling.*

Captain John E. Mallowes was only thirty-four years old. He was survived by a young son, Isaac B., born in 1853. His wife, Lucina (Withington) had died in 1856 and she was buried in Chatham's Seaside Cemetery. Isaac died when he was a teenager.

# JAMES H. KENT
## (1841–1898)
### *An Earl as First Mate*

Edwin F. Eldredge's unpublished *Chatham Sea Captains* only includes Captain James H. Kent's connection with the young Earl of Aberdeen, also known as George Osborne. That surely does not do justice to a sea captain who spent five decades at sea. The year 1870 was the one in which Captain Kent was master of the three-masted schooner *Hera* out of Boston and had as mate one George Osborne, a young Scotsman.

The vessel was bound for Australia. Seven days out of port during a severe storm, Osborne and the captain were both washed overboard. Although all hands were able to save Captain Kent, all efforts to bring Osborne on board failed and he was drowned. When the *Hera* arrived at Melbourne, "the tidings of the loss of the mate were transmitted home in connection with the announcement of the arrival." The report of Osborne's death soon revealed he had been using an alias. We quote from the *Yarmouth Register*, dated December 17, 1870:

> *Of course it was generally conceded to be a melancholy event, but as no one here had any acquaintance with the unfortunate man, after a short time very little was thought of it. Subsequently…a commissioner from Scotland, a legal gentleman, and the tutor of the young Earl [of Aberdeen], are satisfied that [Osborne] and the mate of the* Hera, *were one and the same person; that since he left home his father and an older brother have deceased, which events would constitute him, were he to be found alive, the bona fide Earl of Aberdeen…the fact of his decease must be legally proved, however, before a younger member of the family can succeed to the Earldom.*
>
> *…An application was made to the collector of customs in Boston for the papers of the Schooner* Hera, *which it was thought would assist in establishing the identity of the mate, George Osborne, with the missing Earl of Aberdeen. The documents, containing a list of the crew that sailed from Boston on the 21ˢᵗ of January of this year, and the*

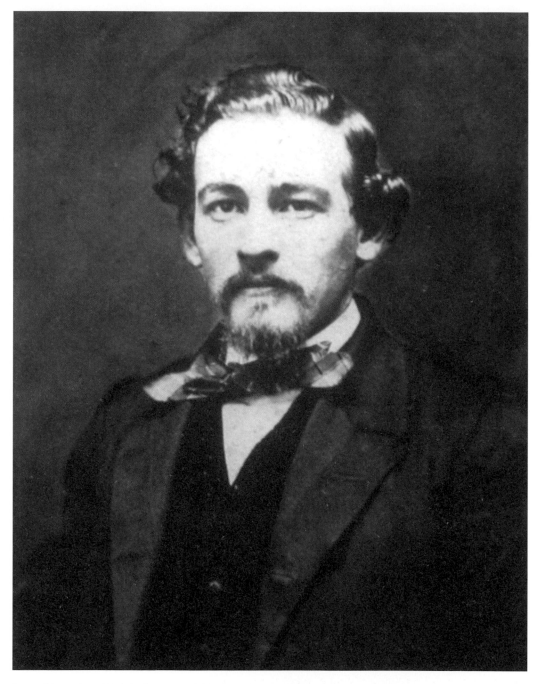

James Kent, circa 1870, before he and his mate George Osborne were washed overboard. Kent was rescued; Osborne was not. The mate's death unveiled the fact that he was the son of a Scottish earl. *Joseph A. Nickerson, Jr. Collection.*

*signature of George Osborne, have been photographed…and will shortly be dispatched to the proper authorities in England.*

It was found that Mate Osborne and the earl were one and the same, though few could understand the young man's reasoning in wanting to hide his true identity. Captain Kent remained as skipper of the *Hera* until 1873, taking her to ports as far distant as Iquque, Peru. Perhaps it was on one of these later South American voyages that his wife Almena accompanied him, for there is a photograph of her taken in Buenos Aires, which would not have been out of the way—a stopover on the passage.

We don't know exactly when James H. Kent went to sea, but by 1864 he was a sea captain. Captain Kent was then master of the British brig *Augusta* of Montreal.[1] A log exists with the brig leaving the Port of Boston bound for Rio Grande do Sol, Brazil. The mate who kept the log was Josiah Nickerson, who began every day's entry with "These 24 hours comes in with…" Breezes of any variety you could name are found, "light, fresh, strong, moderate," and appropriate weather conditions such as "fresh gales, strong winds, light winds, pleasant gales, pleasant weather, light baffling winds, [and just plain] calm."

By March 12, the brig had arrived in Brazil with a substantial cargo to be unloaded. A pilot came on board and the *Augusta* proceeded up the river, coming to anchor off St. Pedro on March 14, "lying in the port Rio Grande North." The log notes barrels of flour were delivered on board, plus a "lighter came alongside and discharged 5,589 ft." of lumber. The *Augusta* was also loaded with about three hundred cases of kerosene plus more lumber. The brig went next to Rio Grande South where packages of woodenware, reams of paper, packages of glassware and thirty cases of furniture were unloaded to a lighter. The vessel, still in port on April 11, discharged 8,131 feet of lumber, later another 6,546 feet of lumber, three barrels of flour and two cases of kerosene oil, "which is all the cargo," according to the log.

Note what the *Augusta* brought back home:

221 salt hides
5,000 horns
hides "from up the lake"
dry hides
4 bales hair
19 bales wool
another 57 bales of wool
and another 3 bales of hair, "which made the cargo."

The date of this last entry is May 12, 1864.

All had not been without incident. Seaman Robert Adere used insulting language to the mate, and another seaman, Charles Teare, who was probably in his cups, was guilty of disorderly conduct and "using insultin langue to the officers." Captain Kent promptly took Seaman Teare before the British counsul. That seemed to provide Teare with a better attitude until a week and a half later when he got into a fight with another sailor during which they "drew knives on each other." That did it! Charles Teare was discharged.

The entry "Brig *Augusta*, Capt. James H. Kent, now bound for New York, May 20, 1864" cites nothing of importance—notes on seeing or passing several ships, brigs, et cetera. The trip seems to have been very long and provisions were beginning to run low, for on July 18, the log reports that at "2 p.m. hove out the boat went on board Barque *George Durkee* bound to New York from Montevedeo got one bbl beef one bbl bread." By July 27, the men were on short rations—"bread about out." They were able to board the schooner *New Zealand* of Brookline and got provisions of clams, flour, potatoes and fish on August 14, two days before the brig arrived in New York.

The log of the bark *Metis*, James H. Kent, master, begins from New York, June 4, 1875, bound to Melbourne, Australia. Like all such accounts, this log is, and properly so, concerned with the winds, the weather, the condition and setting of the sails and the like. An occasional snippet such as "at 4 pm whaleing Captain come on board spoked until 8 pm" or, on Monday, July 12, "spoke[2] a Swedish bark from China for the Chanial." The log writer, usually the first mate or first officer, in this instance R.E. Howes, used the phrase, "This day comes in with…light air, fine weather, passing clouds" and the like.

From Melbourne, the *Metis* went to Newcastle and, naturally, took on coal—tons and tons and tons of it. Then the vessel was bound for Hong Kong. The log read:

> On Tuesday, December 7th came to Stewart Island where under our lee bow at 4 pm six canous (canoes) with natives came along side to trade pigs shells caconuts etc for tobacco and left us at 6 pm.

The schooner arrived at Hong Kong on December 15.

There the Newcastle coal, all 590 tons of it, was delivered, and ballast supplanted the coal, although there was not as much tonnage of ballast. From Hong Kong the schooner was bound for Manila. All was routine until Tuesday, March 14, 1876, when the bark went aground about six miles from Calamba in the Philippines. There are pages and pages in the log telling of the tremendous efforts and drastic measures made by everybody on board and in the area to get the *Metis* off the rocks, but the ocean had other plans. Despite all the heroic efforts, the *Metis* was simply *not* going to budge! The log entry for Tuesday, March 28, 1876 reads:

> This day comes in with fine weather and light breeze from NW with long heavy swell turned to at 5:30 am washed decks at 8:45 am Capt came with steamer and anchored outside of ship schooner hauled along side of steamer put ships tackerling on board turned two sailors and sent every thing moveable on board steamer by ships boats that we could carry at about 7 pm took sailors dunnage [belongings] and all hands went on board steamer made boats fast astern and started for Manila by steamer at the time of leaving a long and heavy swell running and bracking alongside of ship left two natives on board ship. So ends.

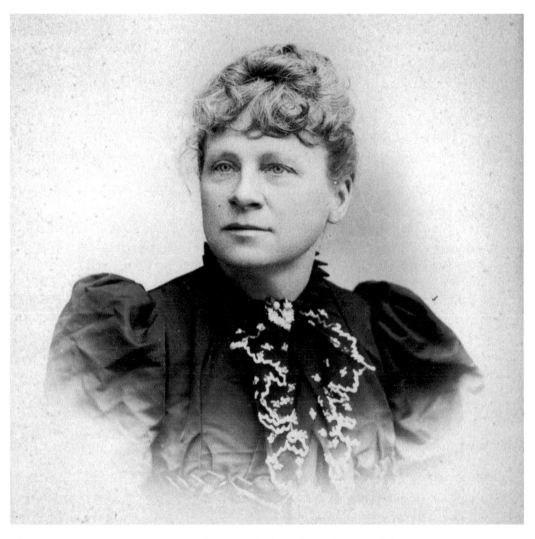

Almena Kent accompanied her husband on several trips to South America. This photo was taken in Buenos Aires. When Josephine Atkins's mother died in 1888, her father asked Almena to raise Josephine and she did. *Joseph A. Nickerson Jr. Collection.*

The log was signed by R.E. Howes, chief officer, Hans Nikkelson, carpenter and George Kellmers, second mate. The following phrase was included:

> *These signatures were made in my presence this 21ˢᵗ day of March, 1876 on board the American barque* Metis *then on the shoal of Palajuia off Iba----Thm. H. Harvey, Marine surveyor to American Lloyds agency.*

This was to provide proof of what had been salvaged for insurance purposes.

One of the later vessels captained by James H. Kent was the bark *James A. Borland,*[3] which left in February 1881 and sailed between Boston and Melbourne, Australia. An article, "Rounding Cape Horn" appeared in the *Cape Cod Item*, quoting the *Chicago Chronicle* of April 29, 1881, written by Alfred J. Doane who was second mate. It told of a voyage beginning in February 1881 where the ship "went round the Horn," as well as what kind of man Captain Kent was. Doane, who had been with Captain Kent for four years and worked his way up from ordinary seaman, wrote:

> *Our bark, the* James A. Borland, *was a staunch clipper built vessel of a 670 tons register, hailing from New York, and commanded by as able a master as ever trod the deck of a ship, a thorough sailor and a perfect gentleman…* [Going around Cape Horn at 2 a.m.]…*A dim shadowy something, I know not what, seemed to rise up out of the blackness ahead. I could not make it out, but instantly it flashed through my brain that it was ice…It lay dead in our course…* [an ice] *berg that towered up higher than our royal yard.*

That they skirted the iceberg safely was evident by another report in the *Cape Cod Item* of a telegram from Boston received in April 1881 telling of the safe arrival of Captain James H. Kent aboard the *James A. Borland* from Australia.

After about four years, the captain left the *James A. Borland*. His last command was at some time after 1884 when he became a squire. He returned to his house and grounds at the corner of Main Street and what is now called "Old Main" where his trees, shrubs and flowers were the envy of all passersby. Dated August 23, 1898, there is the following account with the headline "Fire and Sudden Death" contained in Edwin F. Eldridge's collection:

> *One if the saddest occurrences we have been called to record for a long time took place Monday morning at 3 o'clock. It was discovered about this time that the barn of Capt. James H. Kent was on fire with the blaze breaking through the roof. The alarm was given and soon there was abundant help on hand who succeeded in saving three horses, one of which was Mr. White's, a summer resident, several carriages and other light materials. The barn was well filled with hay and grain, all of which were burned. Two hogs, a flock of poultry and sundry farming implements were lost. A hose from the windmill standing near served to save the house and no doubt several other houses near by. The saddest part of this misfortune is that Capt. Kent fell dead during the fire from supposed heart disease from which he had been more or less troubled. Capt. Kent was formerly a successful sea captain. For a number of years past he has employed himself about his place farming in a small way and keeping his premises in good condition, making his place attractive and inviting. He was an Odd Fellow and joined in the procession on Sunday in the service in the church. Capt. Kent leaves a widow but no children. The origin of the fire is supposed to be from spontaneous combustion. There was some insurance on the building.*

The authors have in their possession the chart chest, which belonged to Captain Kent and accompanied him on all his travels. His wife, Almena Kent, survived him by twenty-six years. Both are buried beside the Charles Jones family in Chatham's Seaside Cemetery.

# ELISHA M. ELDREDGE
## (1842–1903)
### *A Model for* Captains Courageous

Rudyard Kipling's *Captains Courageous* owes a great deal to Captain Elisha Morton Eldredge, even though the two men never met! Kipling never sailed on the Banks, had seen only a few vessels in port and made a trip of only a few hours to Gloucester from his Boston area home. How, then, could Kipling write such realistic stories?

Many of the vivid details of life on the Grand Banks schooners, with their captains and crews fishing the Blue Water, were furnished by a mutual friend, Dr. James Conland. Young James Conland was twelve years old when Captain Eldredge took him on a fishing voyage and brought him home as a kind of protégé. James's father, an Irishman, had gone to California sometime in the 1850s during the gold rush and was never heard from again. His mother, a Scotswoman, had been a housekeeper, but after her death James was forced to fend for himself. Thus, when Captain Eldredge found him to be an orphan, he took the lad into his home.

James earned enough in summer to enable him to attend school in the winter. He was especially bright, so much so that his teachers gave him additional instruction in the evenings. At about age seventeen, he had saved enough to enroll in Wilbraham Academy, proceeding to medical school in Brattleboro, Vermont, where he decided to set up his practice.

It was to Brattleboro also that Kipling and his young American wife came to live. When Kipling's wife gave birth it was Dr. Conland who was called to officiate. This was the beginning of a close friendship between the two men, and it was Dr. Conland who urged Kipling to go with him to Gloucester to taste the salty flavor of that busy port.

The catalyst for the book was the doctor's love and knowledge of the sea—kept alive, no doubt, by his regular visits with his wife and son to Chatham to see the Eldredge family that had "adopted" him. Kipling had access to the vivid memory and equally colorful talk of Dr. Conland. Kipling once said, "My part was the writing; his the details."[1] *Captains Courageous* is dedicated to Dr. Conland.

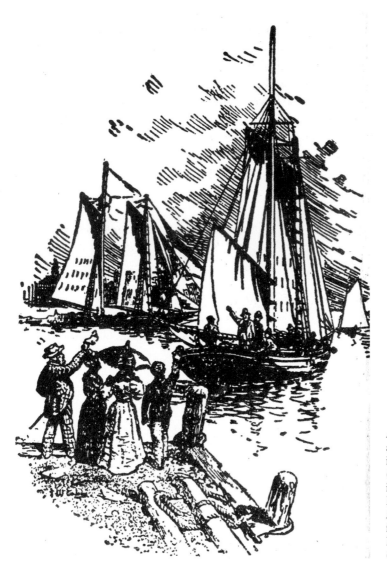

An illustration from an article about Kipling's inspiration for his book *Captains Courageous*, which immortalized Captain Eldredge's schooner, the *Lucy Holmes*, and chronicled fishing on the Grand Banks. *Joseph A. Nickerson Jr. Collection.*

In real life, Captain Elisha was associated with two schooners of which he was master: the *Anna Eldredge*, named for his mother, and the *Lucy Holmes*, named for the shipbuilder's daughter. Edward Holmes was a master builder, a skill he inherited from his father Joseph. When the *Anna Eldredge* was completed in 1864, she cost nine thousand dollars. Captain Elisha was master on her first voyage, fishing on the Grand Banks, plus on the next voyage to Malaga, and then to the Bahamas. Several other voyages were made to the West Indies, with fishing trips to the Banks in between. Captain Eldredge commanded her until 1866 when she was sold for ten thousand dollars.

No plans or pictures of the schooner *Lucy Holmes* exist, but Kipling makes mention of her in his book providing for her immortality. Captain Elisha M. Eldredge was her first master when she was new in 1867, and later his nephew, Captain Clement Eldredge, took command and remained skipper until she changed hands around 1874. The schooner was used for fishing on the Banks as well as trips to the West Indies, where her cargo probably consisted of salt-cured fish, with sugar and rum on the return trip.

During the winter, Captain Eldredge was a grocery store keeper in South Chatham when he was not going to sea. In his later years, he was in partnership with Captain A.F. Cahoon, maintaining an interest in the store until his death. In 1898, he was appointed postmaster for South Chatham by President McKinley himself. He was also a contributing reporter for many years with the *Harwich Independent.*

The captain must have been a strict, no-nonsense father. He obviously didn't coddle his children, as noted in the *Yarmouth Register* in June 1889:

> *Messrs. Albert M. and Harold L., sons of Elisha M. Eldredge graduated from Chatham High School on the 21st. They have walked to and from school a distance of 4 miles winter and summer for four years.*

Captain Eldredge died at his South Chatham home on May 9, 1903, after a long illness. He was survived by his wife Hope and his two sons. Both the captain and his wife, who lived until 1925, are interred in Bethel Cemetery in South Chatham.

# JOSEPH ATKINS
## (1845–1900)
### *A Tragic Life and Death*

Captain Joseph Atkins's father and brother were sea captains, so he went to sea at an early age. When he was twenty-two years old, he sailed with his older cousin, Captain Jonathan B. Atkins, as first mate of the *Sarah* during 1867 and 1868. The ship traveled to the "Down Under"[1] and San Francisco out of Boston. Joseph Atkins described the cargo to be taken from San Francisco to Boston as hides, bales of rugs and four tons of quicksilver, the latter put "into the fore hold to trim the ship."

When Jonathan left the *Sarah* in June 1868, Joseph became its captain. In 1874, he became master of the bark *Horatio Sprague*. The ship was active in the "China Trade," with voyages lasting two or more years. We have letters written from the *Horatio Sprague*. Dated May 1874 from Hong Kong, this letter was addressed to his sister Mary Hammond:

> *I have not got any news to write until I hear from home. We are going to San Francisco from here and hope to hear from you. I would like to hear from the boys* [his nephews] *at any time. I wish I had one of them on board here it would be a good chance for them if they wish to go to Sea.*

Another letter written on the same date, this time to his niece Evie, tells of his experiences:

> *We passed some of the Solomon Islands on our passage up here from Australia and obtained from them Cocoanuts & Breadfruit, also Bow, Arrows and Spears, all of which are rare specimens of their ingenuity. We were very glad to get out from them for they are all cannibals and devour human flesh. One boat came around with their war implements and seemed ready to put them in use. Fortunate for us we got a little breeze and sailed out there from them, for had we been becalmed longer there would have been mischief. One*

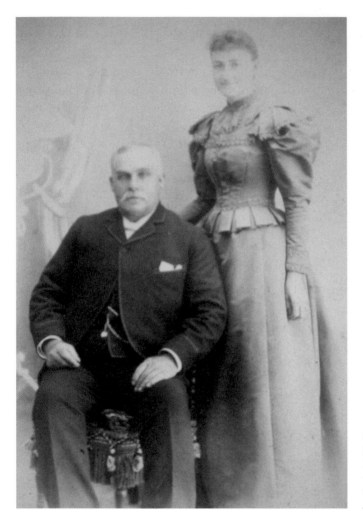

Captain Joseph Atkins is shown here with his second wife Sarah Nickerson. This photograph was probably taken to mark their marriage in 1894. *Joseph A. Nickerson Jr. Collection.*

*Island we stopped at we found the natives peaceful, quite anxious to trade. We got shells &c. in return for Tobacco. Those tropical Islands of the Pacific are perfect Gardens, covered with all Kinds of Fruit all of which grows uncultivated.*

A May 1876 news article mentions that he had recently arrived home from Europe, and after just a few days, he departed for another voyage. This may have been when a harrowing experience occurred. Captain Atkins was in Port Chalmers, New Zealand. While waiting for his vessel to be loaded he went with a friend into the countryside. A tornado came upon them with violent water and wind. He and his friend watched in horror as the man's house floated down the river with his wife and their infant baby clinging to the wreckage. The wife's screams could barely be heard above the roar of the fast moving waters, carrying mother and child out to sea. The distraught father pleaded with Captain Atkins, whom he knew was an excellent shot, to put the two out of their misery. He thrust a revolver into the captain's hands. Only when all hope of saving the two was gone did Captain Atkins use the weapon. He felled his friend's loved ones with a single shot.

He married Elizabeth (Lizzie) Payne of Chatham in 1878.[2] She was eighteen years old and he was thirty-two. The new Mrs. Atkins sailed with her husband to Australia, probably in the *Eyvor*, a clipper ship of the fleet belonging to Mailor & Quereau of New York.[3] The couple returned to Chatham in May 1882.

Their daughter, Josephine, was born on July 4, 1887, and shortly afterward Lizzie became ill. In 1888, Boston physicians found that she was suffering from a brain tumor. Sadly, she died the following November, leaving two-year-old Josephine motherless. Because Captain Atkins was constantly at sea, he arranged with his cousin, Captain James H. Kent, and James's wife, Almena, to become Josephine's guardians. It was the Kents who saw to her upbringing and education, provided for her necessities and taught her the social graces.

Our captain left Chatham to work in Mexico for three and half years for J.H. Hampson during the construction of the Tampico Jetties. He was in charge of all the floating equipment. A letter dated November 1892, written to his cousin's wife Almena Kent while Captain Joseph was still in Tampico, reads:

> [H]*ave a little time to write. We have finished repairing the Boats and Barges. It looks then that I shall soon get a chance to come home. They will not start other work until next spring…but Mr. Hampson says he wants me to stay awhile, so long as they want me I better stay. There are many Americans here…I like this place and it seems quite homelike but I want to get home and see my little Josephine, but I know it is my duty to stay and see this out in order to get another job. I am working for heavy people and they can do much for me. I guess they could get along without me but I can't without them…How am I going to get through the world without Lizzie? I don't live I only exist. So long as I can work from early morn until late I get along but soon as I get Leisure I get lonely. I want Josephine to stay with you as long as you will keep her. Her Mama would want her there and you know just how she wanted her brought up.*

Captain Joseph Atkins married a second time, in 1894, to Sarah Nickerson. This was shortly after his return from Tampico, Mexico. During this period, Atkins conceived of the idea to design scows that could be emptied by opening the bottom instead of throwing the dredged material over the side, and he took steps to protect his design. He was in the process of receiving patents for this scow design at the time of his death, which was reported in the *Yarmouth Register* of April 28, 1900:

> On Wednesday morning, Captain Joseph Atkins, much respected resident of Chatham and a former ship captain committed suicide by shooting. During the past three years he had been engaged as a merchant here and had also been employed in building government breakwaters, having only recently patented a dumping scow. He left his home as usual and went a half-mile away, where he was born 55 years ago, and shot himself through the head. No cause is known for the act. He leaves a widow and one daughter.

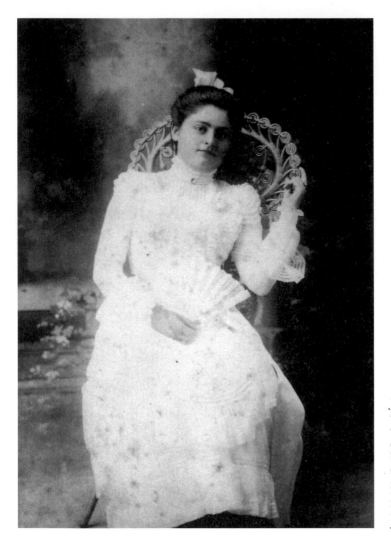

Josephine Atkins became the ward of Captain James Kent when her mother died. She created a collection marking both his and her father's China trade involvement, now housed in the Atwood House Museum's Atkins-Kent Gallery. *Joseph A. Nickerson Jr. Collection.*

His daughter, Josephine Atkins, became an expert on the China Trade furnishings that both her father and her guardian, Captain James Kent, brought from the Orient. Her collection is exhibited in the Atkins-Kent Gallery at the Atwood House Museum. Josephine Atkins died in 1974 and is buried in People's Cemetery, Chatham, where her father, mother and stepmother are also interred.

# Part III
## Sailing into the Twentieth Century

# REUBEN C. TAYLOR III
## (1832–1911)
### *Following in the Family Business*

Having a grandfather and a father with the same name as yours was responsibility enough for a young man to live up to, but to follow them to sea as a captain was a double whammy! Such was Reuben Collins Taylor's fate. As you will see, Captain Reuben was more than capable of fulfilling family expectations.

On September 6, 1871, Zemira Kendrick sold his one thirty-second share of the two-masted schooner *Lottie* to Reuben C. Taylor of Chatham for the princely sum of two hundred dollars. That included the proportionate share of the mast, bowsprit, sails, boat, anchors, cables and all other necessaries belonging to the vessel. Reuben's older brother Levi was her master at that time, according to the Articles of Enrollment dated 1870. In time, Reuben became skipper of the *Lottie*. She was a packet in the coastal trade and sailed between Boston and Philadelphia for Boston's Dispatch Line. There is a small newspaper brief, dated August 1, 1879, which reports that the schooner *Lottie*, with Captain R.C. Taylor, made the passage from Boston to Philadelphia in the record time of seventy hours from wharf to wharf.

Brothers Reuben and Levi had a three-masted schooner constructed in 1883. The *W.E. & W.L. Tuck* was a four-hundred-ton beauty, built for running as a coaster. Reuben was her first skipper. The account of the launching of the *W.E. & W.L. Tuck* is interesting as historical fact but also fun to read as an example of the journalistic style of 1883. This account is from the *Cape Cod Item* in the June 1, 1883 issue, taken from the *Boston Herald*:

> *Messrs R. Crosbie & Son launched from their yard at Harbor View this noon the three-masted Schooner* W.E. & W.L. Tuck. *About 100 ladies and gentlemen went down from this city to attend the launch, and a large number from the neighborhood witnessed it from the shore. At 12 o'clock active preparations for the event began, and at 12:10 o'clock the vessel glided gently into the water. As the schooner slipped gently from the ways*

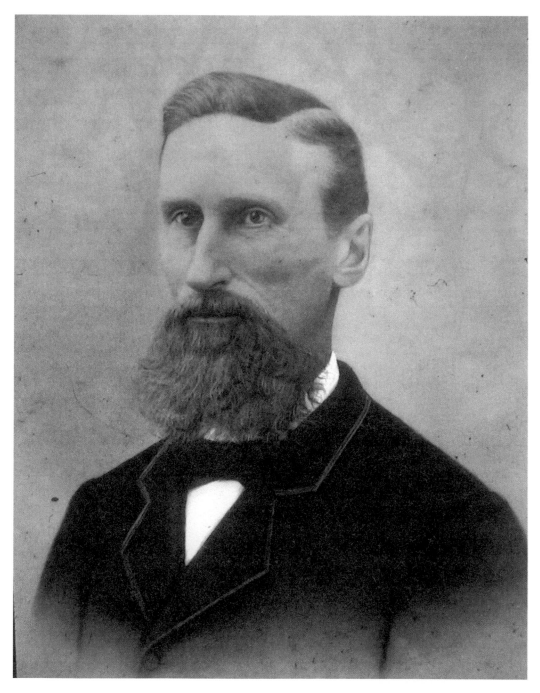

Captain Reuben C. Taylor III and his brother Levi commissioned the schooner *W.E. & W.L. Tuck* to be built in 1883. Reuben was her first skipper and continued as her master until his retirement in 1901. *Joseph A. Nickerson Jr. Collection.*

*the customary bottle of champagne was broken over the bows by Miss M.E. Johnson, and the vessel was duly christened. The tug,* Cottingham, *was on hand and making fast towed the schooner to the south side of T wharf, where sails will be bent and the finishing completed. The schooner measures 135 feet keel, 160 feet over all, 34 feet beam and has a depth of hold of 13 ½ feet. She is built of the best hard pine, and is 750 tons carrying capacity. She is owned by Capt. Levi Taylor, and will be engaged in general coasting trade, Capt. R.C. Taylor will command her. She was built under the supervision of Capt. Candage, and rates A1 for 15 years in the New York Shipmasters' Association. Her interior fittings are on a very liberal scale for a coasting vessel, the cabin being neatly grained, handsomely carpeted and furnished throughout. Quarters for the crew are situated forward, and are exceedingly comfortable and convenient. During the trip from Harbor View to this city a substantial lunch was served.*

In the authors' archives, there are many copies of transactions, enrollments, cash settlements and the like that make for interesting reading. One finds that many people invested in vessels and their cargoes. While the majority of them were gentlemen, ladies also bought shares. At the end of each voyage, reckonings were made after the sale of the cargo. Each investor signed his name in person, acknowledging receipt of the stipulated amount, according to how much he had invested. There were sometimes as many as two dozen, whose claims ranged from one sixty-fourth share to fourteen sixty-fourths. As time went on, Captain Reuben gradually bought out some investors, thus becoming the majority owner/captain.

Only one instance is known of the *Tuck* meeting with serious trouble. That occurred when a telegram was received from the captain saying that his schooner had both masts carried away by lightning in a squall.[1] The ship was fifteen miles south of Barnegat[2]— "sails torn in tatters and masts in falling had torn away the rail, etc." She was towed to New York for repair. Captain Reuben continued as master of the schooner until his retirement early in the twentieth century. Clearly, the *Tuck* was "his" vessel and he was comfortable with her, as good friends may well be!

While a young man, Reuben Taylor had married his sweetheart, Clarissa Nickerson, in February 1855. Clarissa died later that year giving birth to twin daughters: Clarina, who married Nelson W. Reynolds, and Sophina, who married Captain Gustavus H. Eldredge. In 1867, Reuben married a second time, to Mrs. Phebe (Gage) Lewis of Dennis, who had a daughter Phebe Lewis. The couple also had a daughter, Mercy E., who completed the family. The captain and his family are interred in Union Cemetery, Chatham.

# DARIUS E. HAMMOND
## (1835–1919)
### *The Lifesaving Packet Captain*

For thirty-two years, Captain Darius Hammond was master of his packet schooner, the *W.H. Lewis*, specifically geared to the rapid delivery of produce. His run was primarily between Chatham and New Bedford. He did some business at Wood's Hole, with freight from there and thence to Long Island Sound.

The following notice appeared in the *Chatham Monitor* of March 23, 1876:

> *We understand the Schooner* W.H. Lewis, *Captain Darius Hammond, will commence running the present week to and from New Bedford for freight.*

Then the following week, the newspaper reports:

> *The Schooner* W.H. Lewis *arrived on her first trip as a packet for New Bedford with a full cargo of merchandise on Monday, making the passage in 7 hours. Those who had freight were well pleased with the promptness with which the goods were received, and find it much better to have all their goods right at hand than to be several days carting them 7 or 8 miles over a hard road. The packet left New Bedford in the morning and by 3 o'clock the merchants were selling their goods from Chatham stores.*

In April, Captain Darius severely injured his leg on board his vessel and while recuperating had Captain Elisha Hammond's son, Albert, take charge of a trip from New Bedford to Chatham. But Captain Darius wasn't out of commission long. On May 11, in the *Chatham Monitor* he places a public notice that states:

> *The subscriber announces to the inhabitants of Chatham and vicinity that he has opened the packet connection between Chatham and New Bedford. By this line, goods can be landed cheaper than by any other route. Goods purchased in Boston are shipped*

*by New Bedford Railroad, or from New York by steamer, and thence by packet to Chatham. The public patronage is solicited.*

*Signed: Darius E. Hammond, Master of the Schooner* Wm. H. Lewis.

The importance of the packet ships in the commerce along the East Coast cannot be discounted. These small but fast ships provided inexpensive transportation of items from overseas and from other regions of the country, as well as to small towns like Chatham, Harwich and others on Cape Cod and along the Atlantic coastline. Shopkeepers were assured prompt deliveries of goods ordered on one trip and delivered on the next.

Our Captain Darius evidently had a relaxed view of life and its pleasures. He carried a large party of eighty-five souls on a picnicking party to the Dennis Woods. Chatham high school students and their teachers were among the company. This was in June 1882, and it sounds like a field trip to celebrate graduation and the end of the school year.

There is no doubt that Captain Hammond was a resourceful man who saw a real need for services that packet ships could provide, allowing him to prosper as well. An item in the *Yarmouth Register*, in May 1885, reports that the good captain "is taking a load of seed oysters, from New Haven to Chatham, to be placed in the waters of Pleasant Bay and the neighboring rivers and ponds."

Before he sold his schooner, Captain Hammond worked with Inspector McMahon of the U.S. Engineer's Office in Newport, Rhode Island, blowing up wrecks at his direction. Shortly after Captain Darius retired from his packet *W.H. Lewis*, an article appeared in the *Boston Globe* on February 9, 1908, entitled "Life-Saving Habit: Record of Chatham Man Capt. Hammond." Excerpts follow:

*Capt. Darius E. Hammond of Chatham, a retired master mariner of 73, who for 32 years commanded the little packet schooner* W.H. Lewis, *trading between Chatham and Long Island Sound ports, has probably saved more lives directly than any other one man in his neighborhood.*

*Capt. Hammond has seemed to have acquired a life-saving habit by always arriving on the spot just in the nick of time, when a moment later would have been too late, and has performed heroic deeds promptly which in present days would entitle him to recognition by the Carnegie hero fund commission…[He] was reluctant to talk for publicity, having just returned from a hard day's work at scallop fishing.*

*Reminded of one occasion, however, when he had saved seven out of ten drowning men, women and children off Hyannis, and for which he had received a certificate of honor from the Massachusetts humane society, Capt. Hammond said: "That occurred in August 1888, when I was bound to Harwichport in the Lewis with my youngest boy, Stillman, as mate, cook and all hands. We had harbored at Hyannis the night before and were running out toward Bishop's light with a fresh northerly breeze when we approached a sailing party that had gone out ahead of us. I had noticed that a 'greeny' seemed to be steering the boat, which was acting queerly, and as we came near them my boy suddenly sung out, 'Father, that boat has capsized.'*

## LIFE-SAVING HABIT.

### Record of Chatham Man, Capt Hammond.

### nce Rescued Seven Out of Ten Drowning Persons.

Capt Darius E. Hammond of Chatham, retired master mariner of 72, who for : years commanded the little packet schooner W. H. Lewis, trading between hatham and Long Island sound ports, as probably saved more lives directly tan any other one man in his neighborhood.

Capt Hammond has seemed to have cquired a life-saving habit by always triving on the spot just in the nick of me, when a moment later would have ean too late, and has performed heroic eeds promptly which in present days would entitle him to recognition by the Carnegie hero fund commission.

He retired from sea going in 1902, and when seen by a Globe reporter recently at his cozy home on Cedar st was reluctant to talk for publicity, having just returned from a hard day's work at scallop fishing.

Reminded of one occasion, however, when he had saved seven out of ten drowning men, women and children off Hyannis, and for which he had received a certificate of honor from the Massachusetts humane society, Capt Hammond said:

"That occurred in August, 1886, when I was bound to Harwichport in the Lewis with my youngest boy, Stillman, as mate, cook and all hands. We had harbored at Hyannis the night before and were running out toward Bishop's light with a fresh northerly breeze when we approached a sailing party that had gone out ahead of us. I had noticed that a "greeny" seemed to be steering the boat, which was acting queerly, and as we came near them my boy suddenly sung out 'Father, that boat has capsized.'

"Fortunately our boat was towing astern, and running around under their lee I jumped into it and rowed toward them, with a small line astern made fast to the Lewis.

"Their boat sank immediately, taking two girls and a boy down with it and leaving seven people struggling in the water.

"Not daring to pull them into the boat for fear of capsizing it I got two clinging to it on each side and then my boy hauled us back to the vessel. Getting those on board I hurried out again and pulled a Mrs Smith into the boat, who was just sinking, also her daughter and a Miss Hallett of Hyannis.

"I worked the schooner back into Hyannis and landed them.

"News of the accident in some way reached the Massachusetts humane society, which recognized my services.

"I recollect that when at anchor in New Haven harbor during the war a boat containing a party of 11 soldiers was capsized in a squall. Eben Harding and I saved them all in our long boat.

"When in the sloop Village Belle at Orient, L. I, in August, 1865, a man named Russell fell overboard, striking the rail with such force that he was probably stunned and did not rise, although I was over the spot in a boat within a minute after he fell. Throwing my bluefish drail out three times, I finally hooked it into his coat and pulled him to the surface apparently dead. We succeeded in bringing him to life that Tuesday evening, but it was Thursday morning before he regained consciousness, the longest time I ever saw a man in a stupor. It was a close call for him and when I met him once, years afterward, he was most grateful.

"In August, 1864, were were anchored

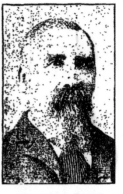

CAPT DARIUS E. HAMMOND
Of Chatham.

The *Boston Globe* celebrated Captain Hammond's "Life-Saving Habit" on his retirement from the sea. In 1908, there was a great interest in the valiant sea captains who were rapidly disappearing from the scene. *Courtesy of the* Boston Globe.

*"Fortunately our boat was towing astern, and running around under their lee I jumped into it and rowed toward them, with a small line astern made fast to the* Lewis.

*"Their boat sank immediately, taking two girls and a boy down with it and leaving seven people struggling in the water. Not daring to pull them into the boat for fear of capsizing it I got two clinging to it on each side and then my boy hauled us back to the vessel. Getting those on board I hurried out again and pulled a Mrs. Smith into the boat, who was just sinking, also her daughter and a Miss Hallett of Hyannis.*

*"I worked the schooner back into Hyannis and landed them."*

Captain Hammond also saved others including a couple and their horse who had fallen from a pier in August 1864. In another rescue, a Mr. Russell fell overboard from the sloop *Village Belle* at Orient, New York, on Long Island in August 1865. He struck the rail with such force that he did not return to the surface. The captain threw his bluefish drail out and finally hooked the man's coat and pulled him into his boat.

In 1869, while sailing down the Connecticut River, the captain was asked for a tow by two men. "Through some mismanagement on their part their boat was capsized, and I luffed to and went after them, and after awhile pulled them both in, completely played out and about ready to go to the bottom," he told the reporter.

The captain also told the *Globe* reporter of a rescue in New Bedford on September 23, 1887. Asleep onboard ship at the dock, the captain awakened to strange noises and hurried on deck to find two men clinging to an overturned boat. It was rolling over due to their frantic efforts to save themselves. Another man was clinging to one of the wharf piles. He hurried to them in his boat and pulled them out. His eldest son Calvin then took the men back to the yacht from which they came after enjoying "too much shore leave." Calvin found the yawl overturned and had to right it too before the captain and his son could go back to sleep.

His final rescue marked the last trip in his schooner before he retired.

> *It seems rather odd, but it happened that on my last voyage in the* Lewis *I had just arrived at Middletown, Conn. And had been made fast to the dock at a lumber yard about 15 minutes, when a man fell overboard almost under our bow. I got to him with my boat just as he came up for the last time, in the nick of time to pull him aboard, and in about half an hour started him up the dock, well sobered off.*

Captain Darius began married life in June 1856, when he wed his sweetheart, Helen Clark. They lived on Cedar Street, in Chatham. Together Helen and Darius produced two sons and four daughters. The sons, Calvin and Stillman, are buried in Seaside Cemetery, as are their parents. There is no record of the daughters' deaths. One can assume they married and moved away from Chatham.

# Joseph C. Harding
## (1850–1927)
### *Master of Sail and Steam*

Captain Joseph Clement Harding, Captain J. Clement Harding, Captain J.C. Harding and Captain Joseph C. are all one and the same man, and he lived comfortably with all of those names. That wasn't his claim to fame, however. It was his command of spectacular five- and six-masted schooners that brought him renown.

His father was Captain Joseph Harding, an important master in his own right, who, with his wife, took little Joseph C. to sea when he was just a tyke of two years. As he grew older, he was fascinated with the sea, and resolved to make it his life's work. At age sixteen, he went to sea as a common seaman—the generally more poetic term is "before the mast"[1]—and in just two years he became second mate on the bark *Chief*. Three years later, he was first mate at age twenty-one. He became master of the *Chief* at age twenty-three, sailing from American ports to the principal ports of Europe.

Several years later, Captain Joseph C. was master of the *John H. Pierson* then the *George Kingman* in foreign trade. On voyages to Europe and the Mediterranean, the cargo could be wood brought from the U.S., kerosene, salt, salted fish and other seafood, cotton and perhaps rice. Returning from Mediterranean ports and North Africa, there most likely would be dried fruits and raisins, nutmeats and oranges as part of the cargo delicacies.

In 1883, Captain J.C. Harding became master of the *Charles L. Pierson* and engaged in the China Trade for seven years. The trade was in coal, wood products, wood for making charcoal and perhaps even ice—all going to the Orient. Returning cargoes from the Orient were varied—silks, chinaware, furniture, spices, et cetera.

The good captain married Mary Eldredge in 1878. She was a natural match for a sea captain. As a sea captain's daughter, she knew the dangers as well as the excitement involved. She could understand her husband's devotion to the sea. Mary accompanied him on voyages to the West Indies, as well as several longer trips to Australia, Europe and China.

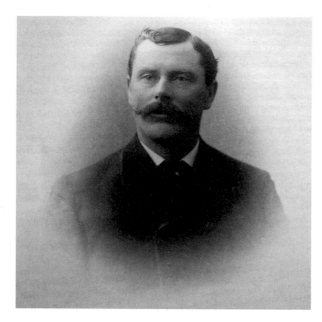

Captain Joseph C. Harding sailed every ocean and was master of every variety of vessel—including five- and six-masted schooners—during sixty-two of his seventy-seven years. *Joseph A. Nickerson Jr. Collection.*

Captain Harding became part owner and skipper of the three-masted schooner *Puritan* in 1890.[2] She, too, was utilized in foreign trade. By this time, the captain and Mary had a five-year-old son, Alfred. Sadly, Mary Harding died at the end of January 1898.

That same year, 1898, Captain Harding became the first master of the five-masted schooner *Nathaniel T. Palmer*, named for the man who built her. She was the sixth and final vessel that Palmer had built for his fleet. In his 1973 book, *American Sailing Coasters of the North Atlantic*, Paul C. Morris recounts:

> *There was a nip and tuck race to see which five-master would have the honor of being listed as the second such vessel launched on the East Coast and the* Palmer *beat her rival, the* John B. Prescott *by only a few weeks.*

The five-masted schooner *Governor Ames* had been built on the East Coast ten years earlier, launched at Waldoboro, Maine, and this was the "ten-year-after" contest, for the honor of being the second five-master in the East.

In 1902, Captain Harding became master of the *John B. Prescott* of Fall River, the rival five-masted schooner mentioned above that actually was completed in 1899. Captain Harding was 120 miles off Cape May, New Jersey, on February 23, 1902, when this vessel met a fearsome northeaster, with snow turning to ice. His vessel foundered in the enormous waves and could not be righted. She was sinking fast when a nearby vessel, seeing the *Prescott's* distress, stood by and was able to rescue the crew and captain. This was the only vessel that Captain Harding ever lost.

The six-masted schooner, *George W. Wells*, was built by Captain John G. Crowley of Taunton and Boston in 1899. She was built under the supervision of one of the leading designers of schooners of his day, John J. Wardwell. Not only was she built like no

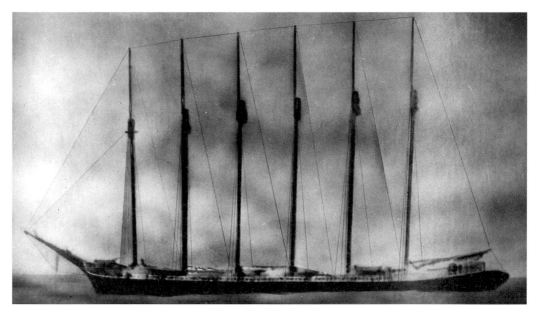

The six-masted schooner *George W. Wells* is shown here just after launching. Captain Harding of South Chatham took charge of her in April 1902. *Courtesy of the Mariners Museum, Newport News, Virginia.*

other in terms of size, tonnage and all those demanding statistical matters, but she had handsome cabins and staterooms finished in fine woods. There were baths, hot and cold water, steam heat, electricity and a telephone that ran to the galley and the engine house. Captain Harding was her master for a little more than a year until his own schooner, the *Dorothy Palmer*, was completed.

The *Dorothy Palmer*, a five-masted schooner, was launched in May 1903 in Waldoboro, Maine. It was said to be the fastest craft of her class. The spread of her sails was two thousand feet. The *Yarmouth Register* as early as February 19, 1898, had reported:

> At one of the large yards in Bath, Me., they are building one of the largest schooners in the world for Capt. (J.) Clement Harding of South Chatham. She is 310 feet over all, her masts are 30 inches through, there being in number five. She will draw 26 feet of water and cost when completed $85,000, and will carry a freight of 4200 tons. She is nearly completed.

The *Dorothy Palmer* was held in great affection by people in Chatham. When she went down on Handkerchief Shoals on March 25, 1923, she was universally mourned. On that day she was heavily laden with coal, drew twenty-six feet of water and, in a severe gale, came aground on the shoals, which were but twenty-three feet deep at high water. The seas were very rough and this wonderful craft eventually broke up into pieces. Such a tragic fate for a gallant, beautiful schooner! Captain Harding had relinquished command of her by that time and was on the West Coast at the time of the wreck.

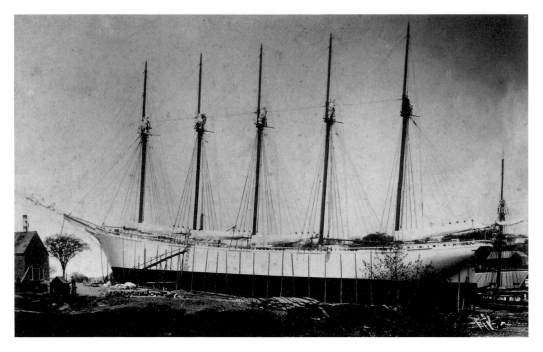

The *Dorothy B. Palmer,* shown here under construction in Bath, Maine, was a five-masted schooner, 310 feet overall, which was built by Captain Harding and launched in May 1903. *Courtesy of the A.M. Barnes Collection, Mainers Museum, Newport News, Virginia.*

By 1922, Captain Harding not only realized that the days of the big schooners were over but he had taken steps to find a steamship to his liking. That was the SS *Algonquin,* which was part of the Standard Transportation Co. out of San Francisco. The Standard's fleet sailed between San Francisco and China. The *Algonquin* was an enormous vessel with a crew of fifty-eight. The *Harwich Independent* reported in October 1922:

> *The many friends of Captain J.C. Harding will be glad to know that in a letter recently received from the Mid-Pacific [Ocean] he states that he is well and enjoying life. Captain Harding is Commander of the Steamship* Algonquin, *one of a line of 12 steamers in the employ of the Standard Transportation Company and sails between San Francisco and China. His home is in Larkspur, a suburb of San Francisco, and he thinks no other state quite equal to California.* [Treason, indeed!]

The last vessel commanded by Captain Harding was the SS *Standard Arrow,* for the Standard Transportation Co. It plied the Pacific from San Francisco to China. For sixty-two years, Captain Harding sailed every ocean on the globe as master of every variety of vessel. He met the hardships as well as the rewards with fortitude and grace.

Captain Joseph Clement Harding and his wife Mary are interred in South Chatham. The finest eulogy that can be given was his: "He was a good man in every sense of the word."

# Notes

## Introduction

1. Alpheus H. Hardy, son of the founder of Alpheus Hardy & Co. of Boston. His remarks were made in 1912 at the Bicentennial Celebration of Chatham's Incorporation.
2. Alpheus Hardy, founder of Boston's Alpheus Hardy & Co. of Boston, to Captain Ephraim Smith.

## Joseph Atwood

1. William Armstrong Fairburn, *Merchant Sail*, vol. 2 *Deep Sea Fishing* (Center Lovell, ME: Fairburn Marine Educational Foundation, 1945–55).
2. A snow (pronounced *snoo*) is a two-masted merchant vessel of the sixteenth through the nineteenth centuries. Resembling a brig and primarily used as a merchant ship, she carried square sails on both masts, but had a small trysail mast, also called a "snowmast." This mast could carry a trysail with a boom, with the luff of the trysail hooped to it. Sometimes, instead of a trysail mast, a snow carried a framework or "horse" on the mainmast, with the luff of the trysail attached to it by rings.
3. Captain Atwood's family was from Eastham. Grandfather Stephen was the patriarch; then there was a succession of Josephs, generation after generation. This Captain Joseph moved to Chatham and married Deborah Sears, daughter of Daniel and Azubah (Collins) Sears, also of Chatham, in 1741.
4. The snow *Judith* was built in 1748 in Scituate, Massachusetts, and her defense against marauders consisted of twenty guns—certainly not a formidable defense against the larger Spanish vessels, with probably twice as many guns.

## Joseph Doane Jr.

1. Quoted directly with permission from Edwin F. Eldredge's unpublished manuscript, *Chatham Ship Captains,* written in 1943. A report also is found in Henry C. Kittredge, *Shipmasters of Cape Cod* (Boston and New York: Houghton Mifflen Co., 1935).

2. In his early years at sea, Captain Doane was master of a fishing schooner, the *Cestus* of Philadelphia, weighing eighty-nine tons. This vessel fished and trawled along the Cape Cod coast and may have been the schooner he commanded in 1772.

3. William C. Smith, *Chatham* (Chatham, MA: The Chatham Historical Society, Inc., fourth edition, 1992).

## Joshua Atkins

1. She was the researcher and genealogist of the Atkins family providing both antecedents and ancestors of the captain, including his family's history.

## Hiram Harding

1. The Boston Marine Society was founded in 1742 and is the oldest association of sea captains in the world. In its 250-plus-year history, its membership has totaled only 2,867 members.

## Elijah Crosby

1. No count was given of the number of seamen employed on board the bark *Chester*.

2. "Wore" means having the vessel move in the opposite direction of tacking.

3. Captain Crosby was also the great grandfather of Jeff Eldredge, the marine artist who painted our book cover and made the line drawings of all the vessels sailed by our captains.

## David H. Crowell

1. The *Barnstable Patriot*, December 10, 1861.

## George Eldridge

1. Peter J. Guthorn, author of *United States Coastal Charts 1783–1861* (Exton, PA: Schiffer Publishing Ltd., 1984).

## John Payne

1. The *Lamplighter* was burned and sunk by the Confederate marauder *Alabama* on October 9, 1862, just two days out from New York carrying a cargo of tobacco to Gibraltar. The vessel was Chatham owned, sailing for the Oakley & Keating Line, and its captain was Orrin V. Harding.

2. Josephine Atkins, John and Reliance Payne's granddaughter by their daughter Lizzie, who married Joseph Atkins years after her parents' death, had another letter that Reliance had written to her sister postmarked and dated from Cebu. This letter is now lost.

3. Mrs. Nancy Eldblom of Potsdam, New York, provided corroborative information about the family. She is a great-granddaughter of Emma Payne, who married Arthur Crosby and then, after his death, she married George Snow, a railway conductor on the Chatham branch of the Cape Cod Railway.

## Josiah Hardy

1. Alpheus Hardy and Ezra Baker were successful coastwise traders in Boston during the 1840s. The firm of Hardy and Baker became Alpheus Hardy & Co. of Boston. It was known for owning many swift ships, including the *Wild Rover* and the three clipper ships mentioned. The firm's barks included the *Daniel Webster*, *Young Turk*, *Kleber*, *Wild Gazelle* and the *Dorcester*.

2. Chatham Town Records, Book #6, p. 87.

3. Grace Hardy was Captain Josiah's granddaughter.

## David Smith

1. Around 1855, he was invited to give a lecture on whaling. A copy of the lecture is in the author's archives. It was delivered as part of a series in Chatham relating to seagoing commerce.

2. On July 2, 1881, at 9:26 a.m., President Garfield was walking through a Washington, D.C., railroad station to board a train. Suddenly two shots rang out. One hit the president's arm and the other lodged in his lower back. Police officers immediately arrested assassin Charles J. Guiteau (1841–1882). The wounded president was taken to the White House to be cared for. Garfield died eighty days later.

## Simeon N. Taylor

1. An Asian wood used for medicinal purposes.

2. The *Canada* was bought by Olyphant & Co. and renamed the *Mississippi*. Some Taylor descendents still have sterling silver flatware with the *Canada* inscription.

3. Washington Taylor, no kin of Simeon but a friend, who had a business in the building—now Monomoy Theatre on Main Street in Chatham, Massachusetts.

## Zenas Nickerson Jr.

1. Carol Wight's *The Wreck of the Velma* is part of the Chatham Historical Society's archives.
2. A synonym for the Atlantic Ocean.

## Horace S. Taylor

1. From one of Dorothea Allen's notebooks: "Captain William T. Savory brought Neesima to Shanghai, transferred him to the American vessel, *Wild Rover*. Neesima gave Capt. Taylor his long sword [probably a Samurai one] in payment for his passage [and to buy a Chinese New Testament]. Worked as cabin boy. The vessel remained in Shanghai until early September, then sailed to Foochoo for lumber to be brought back to Shanghai, then to Hong Kong, at Manila, got cargo of hemp for homeward voyage April 1865. Took 4 months to reach Boston."
2. The bark *Young Greek* was smaller at 462 tons than the *Wild Rover*, a 1,100-ton bark. The *Young Greek* was built in Medford, Massachusetts, in 1855.

## James H. Kent

1. During the Civil War, American shipowners often registered their ships in other countries so their ships and cargoes would not fall victim to the Confederate raiders. The *Augusta* may have been one of these ships, sailing out of Canada for further protection.
2. "Spoke" means hailed or signaled with flags. "Chanial" refers to the Channel Islands.
3. The bark *James A. Borland* was built by William H. Webb for the S.W. Lewis & Company in 1869. She was wrecked on Tugidak Island, Alaska, in 1896.

## Elisha M. Eldredge

1. Philip Jenkin, "The Cape Connection in Kipling's Classic," *Sunday Cape Cod Times*, October 9, 1983.

## Joseph Atkins

1. The "Down Under" during these times meant both Australia and New Zealand.
2. Lizzie Payne was the daughter of Captain John Payne who was lost at sea in 1864 aboard the *Madelia*.
3. The firm's Kangaroo Line, so called, "guaranteed the delivery of goods in first class order and in quick time."

## Reuben C. Taylor III

1. Reported in the *Yarmouth Register*, June 5, 1890.
2. Barnegat Lighthouse on Long Beach Island, New Jersey.

## Joseph C. Harding

1. A nautical term referring to common sailors because they live in the forecastle, forward of the foremast.
2. Simeon L. Deyo, *History of Barnstable County, Massachusetts 1620–1637, 1686–1890* (New York: Blake, 1890).

# INDEX